MARTHA STEWART'S
ORGANIZING

To all of us who want to live fulfilling lives but need just a bit of help
organizing everything that will help us attain that goal.

Library of Congress Cataloging-in-Publication Data is available.

ISBN 978-1-328-50825-6

ISBN 978-1-328-50669-6 (ebook)

Printed in China

MM 10 9 8 7 6 5 4 3 2 1

MARTHA STEWART'S
ORGANIZING

THE MANUAL FOR BRINGING ORDER TO YOUR LIFE, HOME & ROUTINES

From the editors of
Martha Stewart

Houghton Mifflin Harcourt
Boston   New York   2020

PRODUCED BY MELCHER MEDIA

CONTENTS

PART ONE
PAGE 12

ORGANIZE YOUR YEAR

JANUARY

FEBRUARY

MARCH

APRIL

MAY

JUNE

JULY

AUGUST

SEPTEMBER

OCTOBER

NOVEMBER

DECEMBER

PART TWO
PAGE 86

ORGANIZE YOUR HOME

ENTRYWAY

KITCHEN

BATHROOM

LIVING ROOM

BEDROOM

LAUNDRY ROOM

HOME OFFICE

KIDS' ROOMS

UTILITY SPACES

PART THREE
PAGE 176

ORGANIZE YOUR ROUTINE

CLEAN

LAUNDER

GARDEN

HOME

COOK

ENTERTAIN

CELEBRATE

KIDS

PETS

WELLNESS

FROM MARTHA

Plenty of advice has been offered in the past few years on the subject of organizing: organizing your life, your family, your daily routine, your schedule, your closets and drawers. Some of it attempts to simplify the process—just discard what doesn't please you, fold everything into tiny packages or put it in small boxes, make lists and pin them to your door or place them on your desk. These are good starting points, but the subject is so much larger and so much more important than that might suggest. An orderly and organized life calls for creating and then sticking to clear rules, pre-set schedules, and to-do lists that are dictated by your own lifestyle and that of your family. This deliberate, individualized approach will save you so much time in the long run when dealing with life's surprises. It will save you from disorganization and leave you free to spend less time on chores, more time for the activities that prove meaningful to you.

In this book we have arranged "living" and "organizing" strategies into a clear format to help guide you, concentrating on the items that have to be done on a regular basis. We begin by looking at the year, breaking down what needs to happen, month by month. I'm a big proponent of keeping a calendar and populating it with every task, appointment, and event, big and small, down to staking the peonies, grooming my dogs, sharpening my kitchen knives, setting up my grandchildren's sailing lessons, and ordering the Thanksgiving turkey. This practice will help you live a more productive and fulfilling life, day in and day out. I certainly couldn't have managed my busy schedule without it.

We then move through the home, room by room (even section by section, and, in the case of the kitchen, drawer by drawer), offering valuable tips you can easily apply to your own living spaces. Lastly, we outline the most common routines—such as cooking, gardening, and cleaning—into manageable steps, with checklists and schedules to help you handle each one efficiently and effectively.

I've shared a wealth of tips and techniques for getting and staying organized in this one book, the culmination of decades of research gathered for *Living* and my TV shows and online videos, as well as through my personal experience. I hope it becomes your own trusted source of organizing wisdom for decades to come.

Martha Stewart

HOW (AND WHY) TO USE THIS BOOK

THERE'S A REASON you are holding this book in your hands. Perhaps you're feeling that there's too much clutter and chaos in your home. Or maybe you'd just like to see your daily life run a bit more smoothly. This book is here to help you get a handle on all of it—to get organized and stay that way. By using the three-part approach laid out in these pages—month by month, room by room, and routine by routine—you'll gain a broad grasp of what you need to do, as well as step-by-step how-tos to help you get it all done.

Big-picture advice is complemented by "projects" that solve common organizing conundrums (such as making a command center, page 90), annotated images to demonstrate by example (page 102, for instance), convenient charts and checklists for managing recurring chores (such as purging the pantry, page 110), and of course "Martha Musts," offering personal best tips on particularly helpful topics.

Start with the monthly calendars in Part One: There you'll find entries for each day. These calendars follow Martha's planner regarding what to do when. Adapt them to your own schedule and lifestyle. They are meant not to overwhelm but to reinforce the idea that doing a little bit at a time can keep you from having to do a whole lot at once—and also to remind you to schedule in the leisure time that helps keep life balanced.

A handful of each month's entries are bolded in the calendar and described in detail on the pages that immediately follow; they fall into color-coded categories (see key, right), which correlate to routines that will be discussed in more depth in Part Three. Seasonal tasks, especially those pertaining to the garden, will depend on where you reside, so adjust those dates and duties accordingly.

Part Two is all about organizing each area of the home. This is where you really take control of your stuff, as well as of the tasks associated with keeping each space in order, using a two-step system: First size up each space to discern its particular needs, and then strategize the storage. Practical, hands-on tips will help you with challenging spots—sinks and counters in the kitchen, shelves and bookcases in the living room, and closets in bedrooms and the entryway.

Finally, Part Three sets forth the supplies, strategies, and schedules for everyday routines (see the color-coded key below),

Category Key

CLEAN

LAUNDER

GARDEN

HOME

COOK

ENTERTAIN

CELEBRATE

KIDS

PETS

WELLNESS

guided by a less-is-best ideology: the fewer the supplies, the less need for storage; fewer steps means organizing gets done faster and stays that way, so you have more time for all the things you'd rather be doing.

There's no right or wrong way to organize your life and home—that's why this book is designed to give you options. For example, when updating your own daily/weekly planner at the start of each month (or the beginning of each year), you can turn to the calendars in Part One for reminders and inspiration. When a particular space (such as the pantry or refrigerator) is in need of a refresh, you can go right to the appropriate guide in Part Two. And if it's time to revamp your cleaning routine or get the kids' schedules back on track, you can flip to those sections in Part Three. Any way you go about it, clear instruction and easy-to-implement expertise are there to help.

ORGANIZING PRINCIPLES AND PROVISIONS

Before making your way through this book, take a few moments to familiarize yourself with the following best practices.

GETTING STARTED

Clutter prevents you from seeing a room's potential. To pare down efficiently and effectively, employ the four-box formula (keep, toss, donate, sell) and the following guidelines, which will also help you maintain the space once it is functioning as it should.

Set realistic goals: Being too ambitious can sabotage the best of intentions. Instead of aiming to put your entire home in order in just two months, spread out the tasks over the year. Rather than digging through decades of paperwork in a single session, set aside an hour or two each day to pore over one year at a time, shredding, recycling, and re-filing as you go. Similarly, don't expect sudden shifts in your everyday routine; recognize that any long-lasting change will take persistence.

Tackle one room or routine at a time: Start with high-traffic areas like the kitchen and bathroom, as this will give you the greatest sense of accomplishment and keep you motivated to go through the remaining rooms. If a whole room is still too daunting, pinpoint one component (kitchen cabinets and drawers, for example) at a time. When evaluating your routines, focus on what's most important first, whether it's cooking or gardening.

Do a little every day: In addition to devoting entire weekends to deeper organizational dives, make an effort to take quick and easy steps throughout the week. This will keep matters from getting too out of hand. You'll find a few time-management tips in Part Three for when you have five, ten, or fifteen minutes; use these as templates for coming up with your own short-order tasks.

Schedule it in: Don't leave organizing to chance. Using the calendars in Part One and schedules in Part Three, block off time in your planner for daily, weekly, monthly, seasonal, and annual to-dos. Set reminders to stave off procrastination. Reward yourself with a spa day or dinner with friends whenever you've ticked all the boxes.

NEXT STEPS

Once you've pared down your belongings, you'll need to establish a system for putting what's left in good order. There's no one-size-fits-all solution, but heeding the principles below will ensure you find what works for you.

Give everything a home: Stowing objects in attractive vessels, hanging items on hooks or peg rails, and even having handy catchall baskets and bins will make for a pulled-together dwelling. Knowing where it all goes also makes it easier to put it all back—particularly important for getting kids to pitch in with the ongoing cleanup.

Group like with like: Sorting different articles by category (e.g., toy trucks in one bin, puzzles in another; hair products on a designated shelf, cosmetics in a drawer divider; metal spatulas in this crock, wooden spoons in that one) will save time and effort when using them and when figuring out where things go.

Keep it where you use it: Storing things where they are most often needed (pots and pans over an island, a mending kit in the laundry room) can shave precious minutes off your everyday chores. Consider frequency of use as well as proximity, putting staple supplies within easy reach and stashing the rest where they aren't taking up valuable space.

Make the most of every inch: This maxim proves helpful no matter a room's size. Exploit the space below a bed or coffee table or above a door or window frame; mine the far reaches of a coat or linen closet; optimize vertical wall space (such as with pegboard, shelves, or towel bars). Use a desk riser to open up space under a computer monitor and an over-the-door rack to create extra storage in a kitchen or bathroom. Add hooks and racks inside kitchen cabinets and doors. Put the side of a refrigerator to work with magnetized systems.

Use multitasking furniture: It's easy to find versatile pieces that help sneak in more storage. Ottomans and chests are great for living rooms or bedrooms, benches and cubbies for entryways or mudrooms. A dresser can double as a nightstand, a chair in the bathroom is seating and spare-towel holder in one. Rolling carts can be parked anywhere and moved as the need arises. Same for a coat tree, which can be relocated to a guest room when its winter shift in the entryway is over.

Create zones: Similar to grouping like with like, visually or mentally assigning different tasks to different parts of a room can help you stay on-task. This could mean dividing a desk into bill-paying, correspondence, and creative stations, or housing garden and lawn tools, sporting gear, and auto supplies in separate zones in a garage.

TOP 10 ORGANIZING ALL-STARS

With these hardworking supplies on hand, taming clutter will be all the easier—and your home all the neater. Orderliness awaits.

1. Bins and Baskets: Clear plastic bins let you see what's inside, perfect for a kid's room or garage (with tight-fitting lids for long-term storage). Fabric bins or woven baskets create harmony in high-traffic areas such as the living room or bathroom; same for attractive totes, which can double as hampers.

2. Food Storage Containers: Airtight, food-safe jars and canisters are a must for decanting bulk purchases and nonperishables in the kitchen. Those made of glass keep the contents visible. Nesting sets are convenient for storing make-aheads and leftovers, and save space when not in use.

3. Labels: There's a label to match every organizing need, including manila tags or peel-and-stick versions; a label maker quickly prints out IDs for spice jars, pantry containers and shelves, file folders, and other household items.

4. Hooks: Wall hooks keep stuff off the floor throughout the home, including the garage and basement. Cup hooks expand storage under shelves or cabinets; S hooks work with pegboards or towel bars. Adhesive hooks offer temporary storage, such as during the holidays.

5. Trays: Use these to group items for a cohesive effect, such as on a coffee table, dresser, or nightstand—and on kitchen counters, bathroom surfaces, and entry consoles (think small caddies for keys and loose change). A larger tray turns an ottoman or bench into a table, for extra storage.

6. Drawer Inserts: Virtually every drawer has its own solution, from mesh inserts for a desk or junk drawer; bamboo inserts for the kitchen; and fabric or Lucite for dressers and closet bins.

7. Shaker-Style Peg Rails: Mount these in a bathroom to hold robes and spare towels, in the entryway to keep jackets and backpacks off the floor, and in a utility room to hang brooms and dustpans.

8. Shelves: Make the most of unused wall space in practically any room with mounted shelves and ledges, choosing the size and style that serve the greatest need.

9. Tension Rods: They're not just for curtains but also for organizing cabinets (horizontally to keep cutting boards upright, for example, or vertically to hang cleaning supplies under a kitchen sink).

10. Lazy Susans: Spices are just the beginning; this old-school spinner will keep other ingredients (in a pantry or refrigerator), toiletries, laundry provisions—you name it—within easy reach.

PART ONE

ORGANIZE YOUR YEAR

No organizing toolkit is complete without a well-tended planner. On the following pages, you'll find Martha's calendars for the year, which address her seasonal tasks and important dates— like when she sharpens the gardening tools, reorganizes her pantries, or hosts a dinner party. Personalize each month with home maintenance to-dos, health care appointments, and special occasions (birthdays and weddings and graduations). You'll see that each day has an entry, but none has too many—because doing a bit every day is the best way to get everything done without getting overwhelmed. We've also made sure to include hiking, apple picking, theatergoing, and other recreational activities, in hopes that you'll add your own favorite diversions—these, after all, are what make everything else worthwhile.

JANUARY

New year, new you, new outlook—this month
is about recharging your health and well-being. Set goals that
matter, such as staying active and connected. Planning
and preparing are also on January's agenda, using
checklists to make sure you cover all the essentials.

SUNDAY	MONDAY	TUESDAY	WEDNESDAY	THURSDAY	FRIDAY	SATURDAY
			NEW YEAR'S DAY (January 1)	**WELLNESS** Establish healthy habits (page 16)	Finish thank-you notes for holiday gifts	**HOME** Review your financial plan for the year (page 16)
CELEBRATE Put away decorations; recycle the Christmas tree (page 17)	Take a yoga or Pilates class	Schedule health and wellness appointments for the entire year	Stock up on or harvest citrus fruit	Buy bedding during annual white sales	Have a family movie or game night by the fire	Start planning summer vacations
COOK Clean and organize your pantry; **focus on whole foods** (page 18)	Check expiration dates on important documents, such as driver's license, car registration, and passport	Buy theater and other tickets for the new season	Be prepared for snow—keep shovels near pathways	Organize holiday photos	Plan your entertaining schedule for the next few months	Take a getaway over the long weekend
Take a hike or go cross-country skiing	**MARTIN LUTHER KING JR. DAY** (third Monday of January)	Clean out closets; donate items to charity	Schedule meeting with accountant for taxes	**GARDEN** Care for houseplants (page 18)	Draft planting plan for spring garden	**CHINESE NEW YEAR*** Make dim sum
COOK Make and freeze stocks (page 19)	Wax older wooden floors, at least once annually	Check firewood supplies; reorder if needed	Finalize spring-break travel plans	Order plants from nurseries for spring; place seed orders	Plant cool-season vegetables in hotter climates	

*CHINESE NEW YEAR Falls between January 21 and February 20, determined by the Chinese lunar calendar.

REVIEW YOUR FINANCIAL PLAN FOR THE YEAR

Prioritize this now, before other distractions set in.

- Schedule an annual-review meeting with your financial planner, if you have one.

- Evaluate short- and long-term savings goals, and determine if you're setting aside enough each month to achieve them.

- Establish, or review, savings (ideally via direct deposit) and expense-tracking systems.

- Order your free annual credit reports and/or sign up for credit monitoring through your bank or credit card provider.

- Review home, car, and medical insurance policies and needs.

- Reassess your investment portfolio.

- Consider increasing 401(k) and retirement plan contributions.

WELLNESS

ESTABLISH HEALTHY HABITS

Your resolve may have faded over the course of the busy year prior, especially during the holidays, but now is the time to start fresh. Make a list of goals for your health and well-being.

1. Rethink what you eat, with a focus on whole foods (page 18).

2. Reevaluate your exercise routine: Look at what's working and what isn't. Schedule sessions with a trainer; sign up for skiing lessons; register for a race in the spring and start training now.

3. Practice mindfulness and meditation: Start with five minutes of deep breathing upon waking and again at the end of the day, using a meaningful word or image as a prompt.

4. Make time for a social life: People who engage with others live longer, happier lives. Take a cooking class with a friend, volunteer at a local museum, or join a running group.

PUT AWAY DECORATIONS

When you take the time to put away decorations in an orderly fashion, they'll be all the easier to put back up again next season—and in the same pristine shape.

LIGHTS: Test string lights, then loop each strand into a neat bundle, wrapping ends around each one (or a cardboard rectangle) to secure. Place each strand in a resealable plastic bag, leaving air inside to act as a cushion; place bags in a bin.

ORNAMENTS: Store ornaments in a segmented cardboard box made for this purpose (sold at home organization stores), or reuse a box from a wine store. First wrap fragile ornaments individually in acid-free tissue paper. Clear plastic storage bins are also convenient and let you see the contents; keep tissue-wrapped ornaments and delicate bows in zippered plastic bags with some air trapped inside for extra padding. Store decorations where humidity and temperature don't fluctuate throughout the year.

RECYCLE THE CHRISTMAS TREE

Take your tree outside: Lay a drop cloth or old sheet on the floor next to the tree, wrap the trunk in a towel, and then wrap the whole tree in the cloth, enclosing all branches. Carry the tree trunk-first through your door to keep branches from catching on the frame and breaking off.

Use it as winter mulch: Rather than leaving your tree curbside, remove its branches with a handsaw, then crisscross them over perennial beds to a thickness of several inches to protect plants from snow and frost; remove in the spring. If you don't need the mulch in your own yard, ask your local sanitation or environmental department if it has a program to supply mulch to local residents.

MARTHA MUST

I like to give money plants (*Pilea peperomioides*) on New Year's Day and as birthday gifts, because they are believed to bring prosperity. Since they are easy to care for and readily produce new "babies," they make lovely first plants for children.

FOCUS ON WHOLE FOODS

January is a good time to clean up your eating habits. Fill your pantry with healthy basics that you can build meals around, such as dried beans, whole grains, and pasta. Keep leafy greens and fresh fruit on hand (and frozen berries—a good, longer-lasting pick). Carve out time each week to plan meals and pack lunches and snacks daily to avoid poor last-minute decisions.

For on-the-go breakfasts, assemble fresh-fruit and yogurt parfaits the night before. To make the superfood smoothie parfait shown here, make a "pudding" of chia seeds soaked in unsweetened coconut milk, maple syrup, and vanilla extract, then layer with fruit and plain yogurt; refrigerate overnight. Top with a green smoothie (this one is spinach and mango).

CARE FOR HOUSEPLANTS

Keep plants healthy in winter with these four tips:

1. Yellow foliage can signal too much watering. Cut off those areas; water when an inch below the surface soil feels dry.

2. Plants lean into sunlight; for more even growth, rotate them a quarter turn clockwise each time you water, or every two or three days, whichever comes first.

3. Indoor heating can dry out some plants. Run a humidifier, or place pots on trays of pebbles and water (not necessary for succulents).

4. Remove mealybugs (white fuzz) using a cotton swab dipped in rubbing alcohol. Cut off stems infested with tiny "brown helmets," known as scale. Red dots mean spider mites; remove with a cold-water rinse.

IN-SEASON PICKS

BELGIAN ENDIVE This tender vegetable works well in salads or braised as a side dish. Choose endive heads with crisp, tightly packed leaves at the market; wrap them in paper towels and then refrigerate in plastic bags for a week or so.

CITRUS These fruits offer bright colors and flavors when they're needed most. Experiment with specialty varieties, such as Meyer lemons and Cara Cara oranges. Choose fragrant, blemish-free fruit that feels heavy for its size. Keep it on the counter for a few days or refrigerate in a plastic bag for a few weeks. Wash if using the zest; zest before juicing.

COOK

MAKE AND FREEZE STOCKS

Pick a chilly weekend to simmer a large pot of chicken or vegetable stock. You can freeze the stock for making sauces, soups, and stews—plus risotto, polenta, and potpies—in the months to come. Follow these tips to demystify the process:

- Make a habit of freezing cooking scraps—vegetable trimmings, cheese rinds, meat and poultry bones—in resealable plastic bags so they will be ready to add to the stockpot for flavor.

- Strain stock (discard solids) and let cool; refrigerate overnight to allow fat to rise to the surface, then skim that off.

- To freeze stock, transfer the cooled broth to a labeled container, leaving space at the top, as liquids expand in the freezer. Or distribute the stock evenly in ice-cube trays and freeze until solid; then pop the cubes into resealable bags. Use the frozen cubes—each one is about three tablespoons—as you would regular stock.

GENTLE REMINDERS

Be a good neighbor to the birds in winter. Supplement scarce natural resources with a mix of peanuts, sunflower seeds, and cracked corn. And keep the birdbath full (a heater will prevent freezing).

Best way to stave off the flu and other seasonal bugs? Wash your hands. Lather for at least 20 seconds—the time it takes to sing "Happy Birthday" twice—and do it often. Especially before eating or preparing food.

Prepare for your annual meeting with your tax accountant: Organize receipts and gather end-of-year bank statements, W-2 forms, and other tax documents in a folder as they arrive in the mail.

MLK Jr. weekend is more than an opportunity for a mid-winter mini break. It's also a great time to contribute to your community. Check out volunteering events in your area, and recommit for the year to social and charitable causes you support.

FEBRUARY

The shortest month of the year often proves to be the chilliest—encouraging fireside reading and luxurious soaks to nourish winter skin. Don't forget to share the love on Valentine's Day by giving a handcrafted sentiment or a delicious baked treat.

For the cookies shown here, see "Bake heart-shaped sweets," page 23.

SUNDAY	MONDAY	TUESDAY	WEDNESDAY	THURSDAY	FRIDAY	SATURDAY
						Reserve restaurant and sitter for Valentine's Day
GROUNDHOG DAY (February 2) Host a Super Bowl party	Sharpen and oil garden tools	Update your social media profiles	Deep-clean your computer and other devices; then maintain with weekly wipe-downs	Start a new knitting project, or finish a tossed-aside one	Find ways to honor Black History Month in your area	**KIDS** **Make Valentine's Day cards** (page 22)
Go snowshoeing or ice skating	Have lawn mower, edger, and weeder serviced	**WELLNESS** **Take a soothing soak** (page 22)	Make freezer-friendly meals	**CELEBRATE** **Bake heart-shaped sweets** (page 23)	**VALENTINE'S DAY** (February 14) **KIDS** **Send love in the lunchbox** (page 23)	Host a crafting afternoon with friends
Shop at antiques shops and estate sales	**PRESIDENTS' DAY** (third Monday of February)	Organize seed packets as they arrive	Roast parsnips and potatoes from the root cellar or market	Purchase stakes and labeling supplies for the garden	Take the kids bowling or indoor rock-climbing	**CLEAN** **Deep-clean bookshelves** (page 24)
Host brunch for friends	Use citrus and fennel—two seasonal stars—in a bright salad	**GARDEN** **Prune trees** (page 24)	Create an inspiration board for your work space	Plant bulbs, annuals, and perennials in hotter climates	Call an old friend you haven't seen in a while, just because	**LAUNDER** **Organize your linen closet** (page 25)

MAKE VALENTINE'S DAY CARDS

You'll need paper, some paint, and just a few folds to create these charming notions.

1. Apply a few strokes of paint to paper—we used vellum, crepe paper, and pages from a drawing pad; let dry. Or simply start with one of your child's existing artworks.

2. Cut out template (page 278) and trace it on your paper; cut out. Write your message on the plain side. Fold accordion-style, along dotted lines, creasing every $3/8$ inch or so. Fold creased paper in half to form tip of heart.

3. Fan out to create the heart's rounded top; secure edges of paper at center with clear tape.

TAKE A SOOTHING SOAK

Turn bathtime into a mini wellness retreat that will cure what ails you. Start with warm (ideally 112°F) water; rehydrate post-soak with a glass of cold water.

For a cold or flu: A few drops of eucalyptus oil, a natural decongestant, can help clear and open sinuses; the oil also has antiviral properties.

For sore muscles: Mustard powder can alleviate stiffness. Use 2 tablespoons each of mustard powder and baking soda.

For eczema: One cup colloidal (finely milled) oatmeal can help relieve itchiness and calm irritation.

KIDS

SEND LOVE IN THE LUNCHBOX

Give your kids a sweet surprise on February 14.

- Instead of just cutting off the crusts of their favorite sandwiches, trim those peanut butter and jellies or grilled cheeses with a heart-shaped cookie cutter.

- Wrap the sandwich hearts in white parchment and tie them with red-and-white twine (or washi tape).

- Include sliced hulled strawberries (they look just like hearts) with plain yogurt alongside for dipping.

CELEBRATE

BAKE HEART-SHAPED SWEETS

No specialty molds are needed to pull off this dessert—just your basic 8-inch round and square pans for baking your favorite chocolate cake batter. Let the cakes cool completely; then, with a serrated knife, even the tops and halve the round cake vertically. Place each round half alongside the adjacent sides of the square cake, leveled-sides down (see diagram on page 278), and frost to finish.

For the cookies on page 20, tint sugar-cookie dough in appropriate shades (pink and red are shown); roll that and chocolate dough out and cut into hearts of assorted sizes, making sure to have matching pairs of each. Sprinkle with sanding sugar (also tinted) if desired before baking. Sandwich cooled cookies with your go-to confectioners' sugar buttercream or raspberry jam.

IN-SEASON PICKS

FENNEL Choose firm bulbs with no brown spots; fronds should be bright green (reserve these for garnishing soups and pasta). Fennel will keep up to three days; wrap in a damp paper towel and store in an airtight container in the refrigerator. Serve raw with citrus in salads, or roasted or sautéed alongside fish or chicken.

NEW POTATOES While most potatoes are kept in cold storage for as long as a year, these tubers are sold soon after they've been harvested. They have thin skin and a light, sweet flavor. Try to pick them one by one for the best quality— avoid any that are green or have cuts or eyes. Store in a cool, dark place and use within three or four days.

PRUNE TREES

When the coldest weather has passed, thin the branches, cut away dead or diseased wood, and shape what's left— this will encourage vigorous growth in spring.

1. Use a sharp saw for clean cuts, and be sure to wear gloves. Cut one-third of the way into the branch you want to remove from underneath, about a foot from the trunk.

2. Next, taking care to stand clear, saw away from the tree trunk, starting about an inch to the right of the first cut, to remove the branch.

3. Don't leave any stubs: Remove the remainder of the branch just next to the joint; stand clear for safety.

CLEAN

DEEP-CLEAN BOOKSHELVES

On a wintry weekend when you're stuck indoors, devote a couple hours to straightening your bookshelves. Begin by removing all volumes and other objects from the shelves, and placing them on a drop cloth or old sheet on the floor. Wipe the shelves with a damp cloth or a dry paint-brush; then, holding books by their spines, gently fan out the pages to remove any dust trapped inside. Vacuum the shelves with the brush-tool attachment. Before returning books to their proper home, sort the titles by author or as desired, such as by subject or by color. Donate anything you no longer want, or share with friends. Deep-clean your bookshelves at least twice a year; ideally, incorporate it into your weekly vacuuming routine once each season.

ORGANIZE YOUR LINEN CLOSET

Organizing bed linens can pose a serious challenge. Here's one method for keeping all the different sets from appearing disheveled when not in use. Inspired by the Japanese art of *furoshiki*, in which fabric parcels are used for a multitude of tasks, from carrying water bottles to gift-giving, this idea is easily executed on laundry day:

Fold each set—pillowcases, top and fitted sheets—and wrap with a square of fabric (1½ yards should do), using like colors to coordinate the sets by room or by sheet size, if desired. The bundles are easy to tote to a closet or other destination, and keep the linens from toppling over on a shelf. (For a similar idea, tuck each set inside a coordinating pillowcase.) Add labels for easy identification by all bed-makers (i.e., kids) as well as houseguests.

GENTLE REMINDERS

Freshen your winter woolens. Hand-wash with gentle detergent (no wringing!), or if necessary, dry-clean, then defuzz with a battery-operated pill remover or fine-tooth comb.

Forget that old habit of idling the car in the driveway: On frigid days, it's better for the engine and the environment to let it warm up while driving. If you park outdoors, try to position the car so the sun will hit the hood in the morning and warm the battery.

Making chicken soup? Pack up some extra in a large glass jar (best for storage and reheating), and bring it to a friend or neighbor who's under the weather.

MARTHA MUST

Each winter I pick a day to thoroughly sharpen my garden tools, first with a mill file or medium-grit sandpaper, then with a sharpening stone, and finishing with linseed or vegetable or even motor oil.

MARCH

With winter winding down, we look forward to forsythia blooming and maple-sugaring time (think pancake breakfasts). The days are getting longer now, inviting us to linger and labor in the garden—or to just get outdoors.

SUNDAY	MONDAY	TUESDAY	WEDNESDAY	THURSDAY	FRIDAY	SATURDAY
Go skiing or hiking	Start seeds for annuals (cutting flowers) and vegetables, or direct-sow in warmer regions	Replenish supply of flea-and-tick and heartworm prevention for pets	Sign up for a strength-training class, or hire a trainer to teach you what to do	Order gravel for driveway and walkways	Give your bike a spring tune-up	**GARDEN** **Begin garden cleanup** (page 28) Perform a soil test
DAYLIGHT SAVINGS TIME (second Sunday of March); set clocks one hour ahead	Test smoke and carbon monoxide alarms monthly. Change the batteries at least twice a year, or as needed	Plant sweet peas	Buy Pacific halibut (now in season)	Schedule post-winter spa treatments	Bake soda bread	**GARDEN** **Fertilize beds and plant crops** (page 28)
COOK **Go maple sugaring; then put maple syrup to good use** (page 29)	Launder pet bedding and winter coats	**ST. PATRICK'S DAY** (March 17) Cook corned beef and cabbage; serve with soda bread	Finalize tax forms; shred documents you no longer need	**FIRST DAY OF SPRING***	**CLEAN** **Deep-clean area rugs** (page 30)	Visit a local museum
WELLNESS **Get off the grid:** Give yourself a device detox (page 30)	String up an outdoor clothesline	Take inventory of spring cleaning supplies; shop for anything that's missing	Replace winter doormats with inexpensive coco mats	**COOK** **Use spring alliums** (page 31)	Host friends for dinner; serve seasonal produce like artichokes and leeks	Check luggage and repair or replace (it's often on sale now)
Invite friends over for pancakes and waffles	Put away winter snow supplies and sports gear	Clean and refill bird feeders; bring them in at night if bears are nearby				

*FIRST DAY OF SPRING Falls during the spring equinox, almost always on March 19, 20, or 21 in the northern hemisphere.

BEGIN GARDEN CLEANUP

- Cut back ornamental grasses left in the garden during winter, before they resprout from the base.

- Rake dead leaves from beds; add them to the compost pile, or shred with your lawn mower (make sure leaves are dry) to use as mulch.

- Once the last frost has passed, remove burlap coverings from shrubs and container plants.

- In southern regions, begin to divide summer- and fall-blooming perennials.

GARDEN

FERTILIZE BEDS AND PLANT CROPS

As soon as the ground has warmed and the grass begins growing again, the soil is ready for testing (page 195), tilling, feeding, and planting.

FERTILIZE: Adding fertilizer to perennial beds now will allow it to break down slowly, providing a more gradual, long-lasting release of nutrients. A 20-5-10 formula (the numbers refer to nitrogen, phosphate, and potassium) is a good all-purpose option, or you can perform a soil test to pinpoint deficiencies and buy the right product for remediation.

PLANT: Direct-sow cool-season vegetables, such as peas, spinach, carrots, and mustard greens, in cold parts of the country. In more temperate locations, plant warm-weather crops including beans, okra, and tomatoes. You can also plant early-season bloomers such as hellebores and irises, plus flowering shrubs like lilacs and hydrangeas.

GO MAPLE SUGARING...

There's a reason maple syrup is known as liquid gold: It takes a full 40 gallons of tree sap to yield a single gallon of syrup. The rich harvest of sap is a hallmark of the coming spring in many cool regions—soon followed by the delightful appearance of the syrup at farmstands. If you have a sugarhouse nearby, you can visit and witness how the sap is collected and distilled down into syrup. All syrups sold to consumers are labeled "Grade A," and classified by color and taste: Golden/Delicate, Amber/Rich, Dark/Robust, and Very Dark/Strong. Any one of these is delicious drizzled over pancakes, waffles, or even ice cream, but you might reach for the strongest for use in recipes.

...THEN PUT MAPLE SYRUP TO GOOD USE

Here are three new ways to bring maple's earthy sweetness to the table.

- **In baking recipes:** Substitute sugar with maple syrup. Use ¾ cup syrup for every 1 cup sugar, and reduce the liquid called for (usually milk) by ¼ cup.

- **For breakfast:** Heat 1 cup syrup until reduced by half. Add 1 cup fresh berries and simmer until soft. Drizzle over pancakes or waffles, or swirl into yogurt or oatmeal.

- **For whipped cream:** Heat 1 cup syrup until reduced by half. Gradually whisk in 2 cups heavy cream; chill well. Whisk to soft peaks; dollop onto pies and other desserts.

IN-SEASON PICKS

ARTICHOKES The flower buds of a thistle plant, artichokes should seem heavy for their size and have fleshy, tightly closed leaves. Refrigerate, sprinkled with water, in a plastic bag for up to five days. Baby artichokes need only be trimmed of their stems before cooking; larger artichokes require more effort—snap off outer leaves, slice off the top one-third of the artichoke with a serrated knife, then snip any remaining spiky tips with kitchen shears (rub cut sides with lemon to prevent browning).

LEEKS When fresh, these delicately flavored alliums have bright green leaves and crisp white bulbs. Wrap them loosely in a plastic bag and keep in the refrigerator's vegetable drawer for a week. Leeks get dirty when growing; trim off the root end, split the leek lengthwise in half, and cut into half-moons (or as directed in a recipe), then wash well in several changes of cool water, swishing to release any grit.

DEEP-CLEAN AREA RUGS

Rugs attract more than their fair share of dust and dirt. In addition to frequent vacuuming, treat them to a once-a-year deep-cleaning.

1. Vacuum rugs on both sides; tackle any pet hair with the brush attachment. The exception is shag rugs, which should only ever be vacuumed on the back side.

2. Take area rugs outdoors and beat them with a rug beater or broom handle.

3. Spot-treat stains—start with plain water and blot with a microfiber cloth. For tougher stains, use a 50-50 solution of plain white vinegar and water, but test for colorfastness first. Synthetics can be hosed down outdoors and allowed to dry; for wool and other delicate or natural fibers, it's safest to schedule a professional cleaning.

4. Rotate rugs seasonally to prevent uneven fading and wear and tear.

GET OFF THE GRID

Make small habit changes to help curb your screen time for good.

1. Give yourself a daily limit—and then stick to it. Track your usage via apps.

2. Avoid technology for the first half hour you are awake and last hour before bed; plus, instill a no-phone rule at mealtimes and employ the do-not-disturb-while-driving function in the car.

3. Engage with a newspaper, book, or magazine rather than reading online media.

4. Instead of logging on to social media, spend that time on a favorite hobby.

5. If you don't need it, don't bring it—your brain knows it's there even when the phone is off.

MARTHA MUST

After the last bloom fades, I repot epiphytic orchids that have outgrown their containers so they will continue to thrive. I carefully remove the plant, loosen the roots (clipping off any dead or shriveled ones), and repot with fresh orchid bark mix.

COOK

USE SPRING ALLIUMS

Early-specimen alliums, which in some places crop up soon after the thaw, will help you lean into the new season even before you've put away your winter coat. They pair especially well with eggs but can enhance all sorts of dishes.

SPRING ONIONS (shown above): Pulled from the ground before the bulbs have formed, these onions have a peppery bite and make a zesty garnish for soups, noodle dishes, and so much more.

CHIVE BLOSSOMS: With edible purple flowers and a delicate flavor, chive blossoms and their slender green stalks are often tossed into salads and pasta dishes.

FRESH GARLIC: With a milder flavor than the mature bulb, fresh garlic is equally good raw or cooked. Green garlic looks like spring onions and can be used the same way.

SCAPES: The flower buds of the garlic plant, scapes must be removed in early spring to allow the familiar bulbs to mature. They have a singular spicy taste and chivelike appearance.

Winter can be hard on wood decks and porch floors. If water is soaking in rather than beading up on wood surfaces, it's time to reseal. First give the wood a thorough cleaning and let dry, then sand any dull areas (and vacuum dust); follow sealer instructions to apply.

Equip entryways with boot trays to catch wet, muddy shoes and boots. For makeshift ones that are a snap to clean, simply set out large sheet pans fitted with cooling racks.

Prepare your bike for the cycling season. Check your tires and inner tubes for damage or cracking, be sure gears and chains are lubricated, and test brakes for squeaks and worn-down pads. If you're not a seasoned cyclist, it's best to make an appointment with a bike pro for a tune-up.

For the eggs shown here, see "Decorate Easter eggs," page 35.

APRIL

This is the season of renewal, when gardens are really springing to life and farmers' markets are reappearing. It's a time for celebrating with Easter dinners and egg hunts, and seder gatherings for Passover. Prepare to welcome all this joy by refreshing your home, inside and out.

SUNDAY	MONDAY	TUESDAY	WEDNESDAY	THURSDAY	FRIDAY	SATURDAY
			APRIL FOOLS' DAY (April 1) Open up the windows and let the fresh air in	LAUNDER **Clean and store winter woolens** (page 34)	Get out supplies for annual spring cleaning; air out down pillows and comforters	HOME **Replace storm windows and screens** (page 34)
Swap out beauty supplies for spring and summer	Dry-clean or wash heavy coats and jackets before storing	Turn on water for outside faucets; bring out garden hoses and check for leaks	**PASSOVER BEGINS AT SUNDOWN***	Have gutters inspected and clean them monthly	**GOOD FRIDAY** (Friday before Easter) Cook cioppino or other fish stew	KIDS **Decorate Easter eggs** (page 35) Make Easter baskets
EASTER* Host an Easter egg hunt	CLEAN **Prepare for spring showers** (page 35)	GARDEN **Grow rhubarb** (page 36)	**TAX DAY** (April 15)	**PASSOVER ENDS AT SUNDOWN**	Edge driveway and garden beds	GARDEN **Plant new trees** (page 36)
COOK **Eat what's in season** (page 37)	Deep-clean washer and dryer	Clean and store humidifiers	CELEBRATE **Honor Earth Day** (page 37)	**RAMADAN BEGINS AT SUNDOWN*** Take a morning hike or run	Take outdoor furniture out of storage and give it a good cleaning	Clean or service air conditioner before summer season
Forage for ramps in the Northeast, or buy some at a farmers' market	Make ramp pesto and pickled ramps	Reorganize garage, moving winter gear to the back, lawn care to the front	Buy graduation presents	Finalize summer vacation plans and rentals		

*PASSOVER Begins on the 15th day of the Hebrew month Nisan, which typically falls in March or April.

*EASTER Occurs on the first Sunday after the first full moon that follows the spring equinox, usually between March 22 and April 25.

*RAMADAN Begins when the crescent moon becomes visible to the naked eye, and marks the start of the ninth month of the lunar Islamic calendar.

CLEAN AND STORE WINTER WOOLENS

Dirt and oils attract wool-eating pests, so hand-wash last season's sweaters, scarves, hats, and mittens before packing them away.

1. First swish garments in cool water (hot can cause shrinkage) with wool detergent (such as Woolite), then rinse well by soaking in a few changes of cool water until the water runs clear.

2. Roll up in a towel—never wring or twist knitwear—to remove excess water, then unroll onto a flat surface; to help sweaters retain their shape, square shoulders and hems, and keep sleeves alongside body.

3. Once items are thoroughly dry, fold them in acid-free tissue paper and stack in a vacuum bag or airtight container, taking care not to overfill. Store in a cool, dry space (no damp basements).

MARTHA MUST

Every Easter I host an egg hunt for children and bake cookies for favors. Rather than spreading each cookie with royal icing as in the past, I now simply dip each one in tinted icing and let the excess drip off before embellishing, saving much time and effort.

REPLACE STORM WINDOWS AND SCREENS

Remove storm windows and clean with an all-purpose solution of equal parts white vinegar and water, wiping with a damp soft cloth and drying with another cloth. Label windows before storing. Before replacing screens, give them a thorough cleaning: Wet screens with a garden hose; scrub lightly with a soft-bristle brush and an all-purpose cleaner that doesn't contain ammonia, as it can discolor aluminum. Rinse the screens well, and let them air-dry before placing them back in the window frames.

As the garden begins to come to life, watch out for tender new shoots of perennials such as peonies and baptisias. When they're still tiny and easy to miss, they are also vulnerable to damage. Mark off flower bed boundaries with bamboo stakes so they won't be trampled.

Minimize clutter on kitchen shelves by sorting and purging your cookbook collection. Any books you no longer use can be donated or given away. Keep in-season books at arm's reach—such as those on grilling and fresh vegetables. Store away winter cookbooks for now.

KIDS

DECORATE EASTER EGGS

These 3-D delights, inspired by the classic sheer Swiss-dot tulle they are displayed on, are easy to decorate using fabric paint. For even dyeing, first submerge eggs in a mixture of two to three tablespoons of white vinegar and one cup of water for a minute or two, then pat dry with paper towels. Dye eggs in desired shades—such as the cheery colors used here—and let dry (a hair dryer will speed this up). Then apply either matching or contrasting-colored dots using fabric puffy-paint markers, sold at craft-supply and fabric stores.

For the eggs on page 32: Dip wooden eggs (sold at craft stores) in liquid fabric dye mixed with boiling water for a couple minutes, moving eggs to dye evenly. Let dry on paper towels.

CLEAN

PREPARE FOR SPRING SHOWERS

Rain boots getting a powdery haze? That's called "bloom," and it occurs naturally on rubber products. You can polish it away with a clean rag and a bit of olive oil. Or, for a longer-lasting shine, try a boot buffer, sold in shoe stores.

GROW RHUBARB

Known as the "pie plant," rhubarb is easy to grow and produces for decades in rich, lightly moist (not sodden) soil and partial sunshine. If your soil is heavy and doesn't drain well, use raised beds. The seeds take too long to get established, so buy—or ask a fellow gardener for—root clumps with at least two pink knobs at the top.

PLANT NEW TREES

How to plant a container-grown tree, in three steps:

1. Using a spade, measure the height of the tree's container to gauge how deep the hole should be; base of trunk should sit 1 inch above ground.

2. Dig a hole that's three to four times the diameter of the tree's container, sloping the sides like a shallow bowl.

3. Carefully slide the tree from the container; scarify if root-bound. Place in the hole and backfill with soil, packing firmly. Water well and top with mulch.

IN-SEASON PICKS

MORELS Highly prized for their deep, earthy flavor, these wild mushrooms may look unusual but taste delicious, simmered or sautéed. (Never eat morels raw as they contain a mildly toxic substance that is destroyed by cooking.) If you come upon them in the market, choose ones with soft, spongy honeycomb caps—avoid any that appear wet. Store in a paper (never plastic) bag in the refrigerator. Right before cooking, soak them in cold water, swish them around, and dry thoroughly on towels.

RAMPS Ramps boast an intense garlic-onion flavor and have a very brief season; look for them at farmers' markets—or, in northeastern states, forage for them in forests and near streams. Ramps will stay fresh in the refrigerator for three to four days, sealed in a few plastic bags. Clean well before using, trimming ends and stripping off the outer layer (like a scallion). Ramps can be grilled, sautéed, or pickled.

EAT WHAT'S IN SEASON

After months of hearty storage produce, preserves, and pricey imports, the bounty of early spring is a revelation. Asparagus, snap peas, and fiddlehead ferns show their fresh green faces right about now, while other tender young things like baby carrots, radishes, and endive are also available. If you don't have your own patch to harvest, start regular trips to the farmers' market, or join a CSA. Prepare these spring beauties simply, as in these crudités: Blanch the green vegetables briefly and just slice the rest. Serve chilled, with nothing more than melted butter, lemon zest, and salt.

CELEBRATE

HONOR EARTH DAY

Besides planting a tree (see opposite), try these ways to support the environment:

- Plant a vegetable garden or pollinator-friendly flower patch.

- Replace incandescent light bulbs with more energy-efficient LEDs.

- Commute on your bike or take public transportation.

- Start a composting bin at home—or find a local place that accepts compost.

- Buy reusable shopping bags and refillable water bottles.

- Volunteer to care for a local park.

- Donate clothing and household items.

- Check out your local drop-off recycling center; they may accept items your curbside service will not pick up.

- Attend an Earth Day celebration (see *earthday.org*).

MAY

This month is when many gardeners go full-tilt—and when hosts throw lawn parties (to show off those peonies) and julep-fueled Derby Day celebrations. It's all a happy lead-in to the unofficial launch of summer: Memorial Day weekend.

ORGANIZE YOUR YEAR
JANUARY
FEBRUARY
MARCH
APRIL
MAY
JUNE
JULY
AUGUST
SEPTEMBER
OCTOBER
NOVEMBER
DECEMBER

SUNDAY	MONDAY	TUESDAY	WEDNESDAY	THURSDAY	FRIDAY	SATURDAY
					MAY DAY (May 1) Organize outdoor potting supplies	CELEBRATE **Make mint juleps** for the Kentucky Derby (page 40)
Clean kitchen appliances	Set up peony supports in the garden	**CINCO DE MAYO** (May 5) Make margaritas	KIDS **Create Mother's Day cards** (page 40)	Plant flowers (annuals, bulbs, perennials) in cooler regions; mulch beds	LAUNDER **Refresh your bed** (page 41)	COOK **Cook with rhubarb** (page 41)
MOTHER'S DAY (second Sunday of May) Host brunch to celebrate Mom	Weed and water garden as needed (page 199)	Go for a hike or run	Make sure all summer camp forms have been submitted	Go birdwatching to see migrating flocks: Check with your local Audubon Society for events	Bring out lawn games; put up the hammock	CLEAN **Ready the grill** (page 42)
HOME **Wash exterior siding** (page 42)	Apply SPF treatment to white and light-colored clothing	Prune flowering plants (do this regularly); cut lilacs for flower arrangements	Get out beach chairs and gear; repair or replace as needed	GARDEN **Grow potted plants** (page 43)	Mow the lawn	Hang the flag to honor fallen heroes
EID AL-FITR* Take an outdoor yoga class	**MEMORIAL DAY** (fourth Monday in May) Have a cookout; see a parade	Make a summer reading list for you and the kids	Purchase and organize canning supplies	Plant beans	Polish copper pots or clean stainless steel ones so they shine	Sign up for a CSA

*EID AL-FITR Occurs on the first day of Shawwal in the Islamic calendar, and marks the end of Ramadan.

CLEAN

READY THE GRILL

Before firing up the grill for the first time each season, give it a good scrubbing. If you use your grill year-round, cleaning should be a part of regular maintenance.

- For gas grills, at least once a year, turn the burners on high, close the lid, and let the grill run for 20 to 40 minutes; turn the burners off when residue is a white-gray ash that can be brushed away easily. Scrub the grates thoroughly. Let the grill cool, then disconnect the propane tank.

- Wash both gas and charcoal grills, removing the grates and drip pans, with dishwashing liquid and warm water and a scrubbing sponge; rinse well with a hose. Let the pieces dry before reassembling. In gas grills, replace any disposable drip pan with a new one.

- With each use, preheat the grill for 10 to 15 minutes. Scrub the hot grates with a brass- or steel-bristle brush. After cooking, scrub the grates again, and incinerate any leftover food.

HOME

WASH EXTERIOR SIDING

- Most siding—wood, aluminum, and vinyl—should be sprayed down with a garden hose twice a year to remove grime. (Always check manufacturer's recommendations.)

- When necessary, scrub extra-dirty areas with a siding or soft-bristle brush and a solution of nonabrasive, biodegradable detergent and water; then rinse well.

- For hard-to-reach spots, use an extension pole and a brush attachment for your hose, or hire a pro.

IN-SEASON PICKS

ENGLISH PEAS Plan to eat or freeze these peas within a few days of buying (or picking), before their sugars turn into starch. Look for plump, bright-green pods; 12 ounces of peas in pods will yield 1 cup shelled peas. To shell them, snap off the tip at the stem end; pull the string down the pod (like with snap peas). Pop out the peas and blanch until tender; cool in ice water. Refrigerate peas in an airtight container for up to three days or freeze for up to three months.

SPRING GREENS Now is the time to savor lettuces and leafy greens before the heat causes them to bolt (or mature) and turn bitter. Look for fresh, crisp leaves; avoid those with wilted tips or yellowing. Wash greens in cold water, swishing to loosen grit, then lift out the greens and drain the water; repeat until the water is clear. Spin-dry, lay the leaves between layers of paper towel, and roll up; refrigerate in a resealable plastic bag for three to five days (longer for sturdy greens).

GARDEN

GROW POTTED PLANTS

Container gardening offers even the lawn-deprived the opportunity to turn a porch or patio into a green oasis. The plants will be vying for nutrients and water in a limited space (unlike when growing in groundsoil), so advance planning and careful tending are important.

■ Choose containers with proper drainage holes, raising them and lining them with gravel. Mix potting soil with organic fertilizer for the most fertile base.

■ Begin with plants, not seeds, so you can experiment with the design before planting. Use a mix of flowers, herbs, and foliage in different shades and shapes.

■ Consider exposure to sunlight in plant selection and pot placement.

GENTLE
REMINDERS

Stock up on sunscreen and protective gear: Wear gloves and a wide-brimmed hat for gardening; invest in UV-protective clothing for outdoor activities; and be sure to apply mineral sunscreen (guarding against both UVA and UVB rays) daily.

Give rooms a quick seasonal refresh. Rearrange furniture for a new perspective on your space; pull upholstered pieces out of direct sunlight to prevent fading (or add slipcovers, which can provide a pop of color); and move art and photos into different spots to highlight new favorites.

Sign up for an open-air class. Check your local parks and recreation department for their seasonal catalog: Many offer creative work-shops, fitness classes, and gardening seminars.

THROW A TAG SALE

Planning ahead is key; as is being prepared to bargain.

- Clean out closets, the garage, the attic, and the basement; sort items you no longer want or need into categories (clothing, appliances, etc.).

- Mark items clearly with a price—or group items of the same price on different tables or in baskets, with a sign.

- Choose a weekend day for the sale, and check local ordinances before posting signs (you may need a permit).

- Try to get your neighbors involved, too. A block-wide sale will attract more customers than a solo venture. Plan to donate some or all of the proceeds to a local charity.

CLEAN

DUST CEILING FANS

Fans help to cut down on air-conditioning costs. Once a week, use a microfiber duster on an extension handle to dust fan blades and fixtures. For a deep-clean: Turn off the fan and stand on a steady ladder. Remove the light fixture cover. Use a soft cloth to apply a cleaner (household cleaner or oil soap for fan blades, glass cleaner for lightbulb covers); dust cool lightbulbs with a dry cloth.

ENTERTAIN

SET UP A SUMMER ENTERTAINING STATION

Get ready for outdoor-party season by stationing an armoire in a convenient spot—such as within easy access of a porch or patio—for holding the essentials. This one was painted inside and out, given a stylish backsplash with mirrored tiles, and custom-fitted with clever storage supplies: bar-glass hanging racks above, adjustable shelving below, with an under-counter slide-out shelf for as-needed prep space, and a towel bar inside the door. Corral smaller items like spoons in vessels that can be carried to the tables; keep baskets and trays for serving and transporting. Once summer is over, simply swap out the linens and other accoutrements for all your fall and winter (indoor) gatherings.

PREP THE KITCHEN FOR IMPROMPTU GATHERINGS

Summer is all about ease—and spur-of-the-moment get-togethers. Be prepared by keeping wine and spirits as well as pantry staples—crackers and crispbreads, nuts and dried fruits, and condiments—on hand. Aged cheeses, olives, and shelf-stable charcuterie abound, even at supermarkets, for a quick-assembly board. Consider stocking some local delicacies, like honey in the comb from nearby beekeepers, as a treat for traveling guests. Arrange it on one serving platter or multiple wooden boards in various shapes and sizes, as done below, for easy passing, and you'll have a guest-worthy presentation in a flash. And for dessert? Pair fresh berries with good-quality dark chocolate and ice cream or sorbet. Done.

HOME

PACK A SUMMER CAR KIT

Adventure awaits! Be prepared for whatever you might come across.

Blanket: to wrap up tag-sale furniture finds or to have a picnic.

Drop cloth: for protecting the trunk when transporting plants and keeping your picnic blanket dry when placed underneath.

Cooler: to transport picnic provisions or fragile tag-sale treasures.

Collapsible organizer: for keeping small items from rolling around in the trunk.

Wipes: for cleaning up sticky accidents.

Hat, sunscreen, and umbrella: so unexpected weather changes don't catch you unprepared.

IN-SEASON PICKS

APRICOTS Peak season for these (and other) stone fruits begins this month and extends into July. Look for common varieties from California such as Tilton, Blenheim, and Castlebrite. Choose fragrant apricots that are fairly firm and have uniform coloring. Keep them at room temperature, and rinse just before eating.

STRAWBERRIES Look for organic, locally grown berries that are brightly colored and plump and uniform in size, with no soft spots. If the berries smell sweet, they will most likely taste sweet, too. Sort and remove any damaged berries as soon as possible. Do not rinse until you are ready to use them. Refrigerate berries in a single layer on a paper towel in a sealed container, for two to three days.

MAKE A BETTER BURGER

It's all about best-quality ingredients and extra touches.

- Choose grass-fed beef that is no more than 85 percent lean; a 50-50 mix of chuck and sirloin produces an extra-juicy burger; or use ground lamb, pork, or salmon (pulsed in a food processor).

- Choose a bun that is strong enough to hold it all together, such as brioche.

- When heating the grill, rub the grates with the cut side of a halved onion dipped in oil, which will add flavor to the meat.

- Always form your own patties and add mix-ins (herbs and spices; chopped raw bacon or pancetta; minced pickles or kimchi; diced chiles or adobo sauce).

KIDS

CRAFT A FATHER'S DAY GIFT

Repurpose a memento from a favorite family vacation into a gift for dear old Dad. To make these coasters:

Place a map face down, preferably on a self-healing cutting mat. Using a craft knife (an adult should do this for younger kids), trace around a cork coaster, sold at craft-supply stores, to cut out circles. Brush glue sealant (such as Mod Podge) on one side of the coaster; adhere it to the back of a map circle, smoothing out any bubbles. Brush the top and sides of the coaster thinly with more glue sealant; let dry. Repeat to make a set.

DISPLAY CHILDREN'S ARTWORK

The end of the school year usually involves being presented with a substantial pile of classroom creations. Rather than tuck them away in an archival box, why not put a handful on display? On a bedroom or hallway wall, frame some choice pieces with painters' tape, which comes in a variety of widths and colors. The tape is low-tack, so you can keep the art exhibition in regular rotation.

GENTLE REMINDERS

Keep the aphid population under control by regularly checking outdoor plants—especially the stems and undersides of leaves, where the bugs like to hide and feed. They're tiny, but you'll often find them in clusters. A blast of cold water from the hose will remove them.

Brush up on food safety: Food shouldn't sit out at room temperature for more than two hours (one hour on 90-plus-degree days). Don't crowd the refrigerator, and invest in appliance thermometers—the refrigerator should be 40 degrees; the freezer, zero.

There's nothing like a refreshing dip during hot weather, but both chlorine and salt water can be hard on swimwear. After each use, rinse out your suit with clean, cool water, squeeze it out gently, and hang it to dry.

MARTHA MUST

When hosting friends for a casual lunch or dinner during the warmer months, I often turn to pasta—it's simple, doesn't require hours at the stove, and showcases vegetables and herbs from my own garden. Estimate two to three ounces of dried pasta per person.

JULY

The season is in full swing now, and all those extra hours of daylight offer plenty of incentive to break from the chores and dive into summer-holiday mode. Preserve the goodness of cherries, pack a picnic, ride a bike, hit the beach, watch fireworks—or just loll in a hammock with a favorite book.

SUNDAY	MONDAY	TUESDAY	WEDNESDAY	THURSDAY	FRIDAY	SATURDAY
			Hang the flag	Stock up on citronella candles	**COOK** **Bake a patriotic pie** (page 52)	**INDEPENDENCE DAY** (July 4) Watch fireworks **PETS** **Keep pets calm** during fireworks (page 52)
ENTERTAIN **Pack a picnic** (page 53)	Plant basil	**COOK** **Pick and freeze blueberries** (page 53)	Stake dahlias	Replenish sunscreen supply	Restock flea-and-tick protection for pets (and always check outdoor pets for ticks)	Host a lawn party with badminton and croquet
GARDEN **Grow tomatoes** (page 54)	Pick herbs; make pesto	Bake fruit tarts	Take in an outdoor movie or concert	Cut hydrangeas for flower arrangements	Feast on fresh Alaskan salmon	Take a garden tour (check your local conservancy)
Host a clambake on the beach, or in your kitchen	Declare this a do-nothing (other than reading and relaxing) day	Savor fresh cherries while they last	Weed and water the garden	Raise lawn-mower blades as grass growth slows	**GARDEN** **Help the bees** (page 54)	Gather friends for a bike ride and breakfast
Go water-skiing or paddleboarding	Schedule back-to-school haircuts for kids	Visit a pick-your-own farm for peaches and plums	Make peach cobbler and peach ice cream	**COOK** **Prepare no-cook meals** (page 55)	Treat your feet to a spa pedicure (it's the height of sandal season)	

KEEP PETS CALM

It just wouldn't be summer without the booms and claps of fireworks and thunderstorms—both top causes of pet anxiety.

- Keep pets inside, and with access to their own safe place.

- If your pet hides, let it stay there; if it wants comfort, offer some, but don't overdo it (and thus reinforce anxiety).

- Remain calm—pets sense your stress.

- Use ambient noise to mask the sounds.

- Invest in a calming jacket such as a ThunderShirt.

- Use aromatherapy oils (Rescue Remedy is one) on bedding and/or the pet's fur.

- Thunderstorms also create static electricity that pets feel long before and after the storm has passed; set the pet in an empty bathtub, which is grounded and acts like a shield, or rub its fur with unscented dryer sheets (do this infrequently).

COOK

BAKE A PATRIOTIC PIE

This Fourth of July, bake your go-to fruit pie in a way that will have your guests seeing stars.

Begin with two disks of pâte brisée: one for the pie plate and the other for the decorations. Chill the disks for at least an hour and preferably overnight before rolling out.

For the stars and stripes: Use different-sized cookie cutters to punch out the stars, and a pastry wheel or knife and a straightedge to cut out stripes. Arrange the cutouts on the pie, brushing the bottoms with egg wash to help them adhere. Freeze the pie for one hour to help the cutouts keep their shape. Brush the top and rim of the pie with egg wash, sprinkle with sanding sugar, and bake on a rimmed baking sheet until the crust is golden brown and the filling is bubbling.

ENTERTAIN

PACK A PICNIC

This summer, rethink the way you set out that spread. When a trip to the park, beach, or outdoor concert venue beckons, use these strategies to create a picnic that's equal parts ease and efficiency. Remember to always keep a blanket in the car—oilcloth ones are resistant to wet grass, or first lay down a drop cloth.

- Flavor meat with herbs rather than wet sauces. Below, the pulled pork was infused with an Italian-style herb-spice paste rather than barbecue sauce.

- For sandwiches, choose sturdy bread, such as crusty ciabatta rolls.

- In lieu of messy coleslaw, bring sliced fennel.

- Buy an assortment of antipasti, such as olives, jarred artichokes, pepperoncini, and chunks of Parmesan cheese, all of which can be speared with toothpicks.

- Premix a batch of cocktails: In a large mason jar, premix 48 ounces lager, 24 ounces ginger beer, 4 ounces Campari, and ⅔ cup fresh lemon juice. Chill for up to an hour in a cooler. Bring plenty of seltzer water for a nonalcoholic beverage.

COOK

PICK AND FREEZE BLUEBERRIES

The fruit is in season April through September, but now is the time to head to a farm for blueberry picking. The superfood spoils quickly, so eat what you can, then make jam (page 223) and freeze the rest: Freeze in a single layer on a rimmed baking sheet until firm (two hours); then transfer to labeled-and-dated freezer bags to carry you through the off-season.

IN-SEASON PICKS

CHERRIES Sweet cherries are great eaten out of hand. Smaller, sour cherries make tasty pies. For both, choose shiny, vibrant fruits that are firm but not hard and have no bruises. Once you get them home, eat or cook with cherries within about four days; in the meantime, store them in the fridge, in an open container. Rinse before eating or using.

TOMATOES Ripe tomatoes will smell sweet and fruity. Choose plump, shiny ones that are heavy for their size and give slightly when gently pressed. They should be free of soft spots or blemishes, although heirloom tomatoes can be less than perfect-looking. Store at room temperature, away from direct sunlight. Once cut, wrap with plastic and refrigerate.

HELP THE BEES

With their populations dropping, it's time to give these important pollinators a helping hand. Honeybees may live in hives, but mason bees don't—and they rarely sting. Invite these solitary citizens to your garden by constructing a bee house out of inexpensive bamboo reeds, available at garden centers. Cut a long (½- to ¾-inch-diameter) piece into several 6-inch lengths using a sharp, fine-tooth pruning saw. Then tie them together with waxed twine, and place the bundle between tree branches for shelter.

GARDEN

GROW TOMATOES

Taking the following steps over the growing season will keep your tomatoes less susceptible to rotting from disease or pests—and they'll get larger and ripen faster.

- As they grow, tie the plants' stems to the stakes every 6 or 8 inches with garden twine.

- Prune leaves from bottom stems near the soil to keep the plant light and airy; also be sure to weed and water regularly (about 2 inches per week, preferably in the morning). Adding rocks to the base will help retain moisture during hot temperatures and times of drought.

- Avoid overfertilizing established plants, which will encourage foliage, not fruit. Every seven to ten days, spray the plant lightly all over with fish emulsion rather than applying it to the soil.

MARTHA MUST

I love using my own herbs to make pesto. Besides the classic basil, Parmesan, and pine nut or walnut version, you can omit the cheese and prepare pesto with parsley, almonds, and orange zest; mint, pistachios, and lemon zest; or cilantro, cashews, and red chiles. I freeze the pesto, topped with more oil, for up to three months.

PREPARE NO-COOK MEALS

It's hot enough without turning on the oven or stove top. Plus, this is the month for peak-of-season summer produce—tomatoes and cucumbers and zucchini and peppers—that will make any store-bought shortcut taste fresh.

Build dinners on heat-free foundations—homemade hummus or guacamole, for example—and pantry staples such as canned beans and tinned fish. Think panzanella made with day-old crusty bread (add chickpeas for protein); gazpacho with precooked shrimp; Middle Eastern wraps with tahini, cucumbers, tomatoes, and vacuum-packed lentils; and (below) an Asian-style bowl with marinated tofu, baby bok choy, no-cook rice noodles (they become tender after soaking in hot water for ten minutes), and an easy sauce made with peanut butter, honey, soy sauce, scallions, and fresh ginger, plus sliced Thai chiles and peanuts for the garnish.

GENTLE REMINDERS

Take advantage of old-fashioned home-cooling techniques. Keep curtains drawn during the hottest part of the day, and at other times open windows and allow cross-breezes to cool the space. Run ceiling fans in occupied rooms—they can make the space feel up to four degrees cooler.

Replant basil early in the month. Most varieties mature in about 70 days, so this planting will be ready around the same time as late-summer tomatoes—a natural pair.

Planning a trip? Enlist a friend or neighbor to look after and water your plants, especially any hanging planters, which can dry out in as little as a day when the weather is hot and dry.

AUGUST

Savor the end of summer with just-picked tomatoes, fresh corn, and other seasonal produce. Enjoy them as pickles or in jam, on a guest-worthy sandwich board, or hot off the grill. Before back-to-school prep begins, take a vacation and spend time with family and friends.

SUNDAY	MONDAY	TUESDAY	WEDNESDAY	THURSDAY	FRIDAY	SATURDAY
						Have car serviced (as needed); check tires and children's car seats before going on a road trip
Go kayaking, canoeing, or for a swim	Make jam (plum, peach, raspberry, tomato, onion)	**ENTERTAIN** **Build a sandwich board** **(page 58)**	Prepare a travel activity kit for kids	**COOK** **Grill corn** **(page 59)**	Harvest vegetables or visit a farmstand	**COOK** **Pack vacation-rental provisions** **(page 59)**
Spend the day—or the week—at the beach	Pickle vegetables (okra, green beans, peppers, cucumbers, zucchini) and watermelon rind	Pick herbs for making cocktails	Host a backyard movie night	**HOME** **Display travel keepsakes** **(page 60)**	Take the kids to an adventure park for zip-lining and more	Go lobstering or freshwater fishing
Get ready for school: Buy school supplies and organize study area	Use a surplus of zucchini: Bake bread, or shave into "noodles" for a pasta substitute	Plant broccoli, cabbage, and other crucifers	**WELLNESS** **Stay hydrated** **(page 60)**	Register kids for fall sports teams and after-school programs	Sharpen and oil garden tools	Take a morning swim or hike
Play tennis (or ping pong) / Update social media profiles	Prune flowering plants (to prolong blooms) / Order bulbs for fall planting	Cool down with an affogato float: Pour espresso over ice cream and top with seltzer	**LAUNDER** **Freshen beach towels** **(page 61)**	Press cuttings from the garden (it's a great activity for even young children)	Confirm post-summer dermatologist appointment	Visit a local state fair, or plan a road trip around one

BUILD A SANDWICH BOARD

Lobster elevates the classic BLT to guest-worthy status—as does the eye-catching presentation. It's an easy feat to pull off, especially if you have a fishmonger steam and remove the meat for you. Using ripe tomatoes in a rainbow of colors is worth a trip to a farmstand, providing excellent bang for your buck. Flank them with boiled eggs, avocado, and basil, plus brioche or pullman bread. Upgrade the condiments: Mix mayo with crisp bacon, and red-wine vinegar with a minced shallot (for a mignonette).

MARTHA MUST

When in Maine, I love boiling fresh-caught lobster. The ones on the smaller side, between 1¼ to 1⅓ pounds, are sweeter than larger lobsters. Rather than dropping them directly into boiling water alive, put them in the freezer for a few minutes to numb them, then sever their spines in one fell swoop. Before serving, clip the claw tips to drain any excess liquid, so it doesn't run onto the plate.

GRILL CORN

Come August, you'll appreciate having some new tips and tricks for cooking corn while it's at its sweet, flavorful peak. Here are a few favorites:

■ For hassle-free husking: Cook unpeeled cobs over indirect heat in a covered grill (about 400°F) for about 30 minutes; the husks will slip right off—silk and all—and the kernels will be perfectly tender. Slice them into salads, salsas, and pastas or eat straight off the cobs.

■ For a twist on the popular Mexican street-cart snack (shown below): Grill husked cobs until lightly charred in spots, slather with mayonnaise, and sprinkle with bacon, oregano, Parmesan, salt, and pepper. Or swap out Parmesan for crumbled feta or goat cheese.

■ For flavorful spreads: In a food processor, pulse a softened stick of butter with chopped herbs and other seasonings: Try mint with Thai red curry paste, chives with white miso paste, cilantro with lime zest and jalapeño chile, thyme and/or rosemary with roasted garlic.

PACK VACATION-RENTAL PROVISIONS

Rentals can often lack basic supplies for preparing meals. Tweak the list below to include your own must-haves:

PANTRY STAPLES
■ kosher salt

■ flaky sea salt

■ ground pepper

■ red-pepper flakes

■ dried oregano

■ dried thyme

■ extra-virgin olive oil

■ coffee/tea

BAKING BASICS
■ all-purpose flour (or a gluten-free blend)

■ baking powder

■ baking soda

■ ground cinnamon

■ pure vanilla extract

ESSENTIAL EQUIPMENT
■ cast-iron skillet

■ chef's knife

■ rasp grater

■ instant thermometer (for grilling meats)

■ dish towels

DISPLAY TRAVEL KEEPSAKES

Summer vacations often involve coming home with a trove of seashells and other finds. Rather than keep the items hidden away or scattered randomly, curate your collection so you can be reminded of your trip every day. Sort different types, each into its own vessel—clear glasses or vases hold tiny treasures; a tray of larger shells can in turn hold paper clips and other desk essentials. Sculptural pieces of coral can serve as decor and spots for business cards, sticky-notes, and other small papers you want to keep in view. Tape or tack up a photo or postcard, and your desk will instantly become your at-home happy place.

STAY HYDRATED

To keep your body humming in summer, replace sugary beverages with infused water: Fill a pitcher of water (preferably filtered) with fresh fruit and herbs—try pineapple, fresh ginger, and mint; or cucumber, lemon, and basil—and refrigerate for several hours to let the flavors meld. With their pretty colors, the refreshers make inviting (no-alcohol) options for parties, too.

IN-SEASON PICKS

CORN Head to a farm or greenmarket for the freshest corn possible. Refrigerate the ears for up to three days to slow down the sugar-to-starch conversion process; leave the husks on, wrap tightly in plastic, and keep in the vegetable crisper. To freeze: Slice kernels from cobs, and freeze them in resealable bags for up to three months. When ready to use, boil until tender.

ZUCCHINI Pick medium- to small-size ones (half a pound each) with smooth, dark-green skin. Store in an open plastic bag in the refrigerator for a week or two. To freeze extra, cut into pieces, blanch, drain, and freeze on a baking sheet until firm, then transfer to airtight plastic bags; use within three months. You can also freeze grated raw zucchini (drain well before storing).

LAUNDER
FRESHEN BEACH TOWELS

After a season of swim and sun, most towels could benefit from a deep clean. Launder them in the washing machine on the hottest setting with a cup of white vinegar. If any chlorine or musty odor lingers, wash them again with $1/2$ cup of baking soda and hot water. A two-step drying process freshens the scent: Tumble-dry towels most of the way on high, for softness; then, when they are just damp, move them to an outdoor clothesline to finish drying.

GENTLE REMINDERS

Now is the time to slow down the garden's growth in preparation for fall. Stop feeding lawns, perennials, and woody plants by mid-month. You want to avoid new growth popping up with too little time to mature before temperatures drop.

Take a run on the beach. It's not only beautiful—running on sand is easier on your joints but also burns more calories than running on pavement. If you aren't used to it, start out on the hard sand closest to the water, and wear shoes. Add barefoot runs, starting off short and working up to longer ones to avoid injury.

Pack travel kits for kids: Keep them occupied during long hours in the car or plane by filling backpacks with activities (see page 259 for a few ideas), ideally ones they haven't seen before: new coloring books, sketch pads and colored pencils, and travel-sized games. Don't forget snacks!

SEPTEMBER

The transition from summer to fall means getting back to basics: freezing big-batch soups for the colder months, preparing the garden for next year's blooms, and reorganizing your pantry and closets. There are also apples to pick and pies to bake.

SUNDAY	MONDAY	TUESDAY	WEDNESDAY	THURSDAY	FRIDAY	SATURDAY
		Organize digital photos from summer	Pick raspberries	Plant cool-weather greens	Schedule winter furnace service before weather turns cold	Go on a road trip for the holiday weekend
Soak up the sun at a beach, lake, or watering hole	**LABOR DAY** (first Monday of September)	Clean fans and store portable ones	GARDEN **Harvest fresh herbs** (page 64)	Update the family calendar with important dates now that school has started	Pick hot peppers and string them to dry; or make hot-pepper jelly	GARDEN **Plant spring bulbs in pots** (page 64)
Visit a local winery during harvest season (now through early October)	CLEAN **Swap out seasonal items** (page 65)	Scrub porch floors, ceiling, and walls	Harvest the last of the tomato crops, then pull up the plants and compost them	Clean and ready all bird feeders for fall and winter; order bird seed from Audubon	**ROSH HASHANAH BEGINS AT SUNDOWN*** (163 days from first day of Passover)	CLEAN **Ready the kitchen for fall** (page 66)
ROSH HASHANAH ENDS AT SUNDOWN Take the family on a hike	Bring potted plants back inside, if necessary	**FIRST DAY OF AUTUMN***	COOK **Prepare a hearty soup** (page 66)	Rake the first fall leaves; aerate and seed the lawn	Divide and plant perennials (bearded iris, hosta, phlox, rudbeckia)	COOK Pick apples; **update apple pie** (page 67)
YOM KIPPUR BEGINS AT SUNDOWN (9 days after the first day of Rosh Hashanah)	**YOM KIPPUR ENDS AT SUNDOWN**	KIDS **Plan ahead for school lunches** (page 67)	Install storm windows			

*ROSH HASHANAH Observed on the first two days of the Hebrew month Tishrei, which can occur anytime between September 5 and October 5.
*FIRST DAY OF AUTUMN Usually falls between September 21 and September 24 in the northern hemisphere.

HARVEST FRESH HERBS

You'll want to clip the last of your summer herbs before the first frost—then use one of the following ways (plus pesto, page 54) to savor their flavor over the months ahead.

DRY (FOR WOODY HERBS): Wrap kitchen twine around the stems and hang them upside down in a cool, dry place for four to ten days, until they are crisp and easily crumbled in your hands. Pick the leaves from the stems and place in a jar; seal—they'll keep for six months.

FREEZE (FOR SOFT HERBS): Chop the leaves and fill an ice-cube tray three-quarters full with them, pressing down to compress; pour in boiling water to cover. Freeze until solid, pop out the cubes, and store in a resealable freezer bag for up to six months. Use in place of regular ice cubes to chill drinks or in soups, too.

PLANT SPRING BULBS IN POTS

For a steady stream of blooms next year, plant bulbs now in pots—in layers. Small, early bloomers go on top, larger ones, planted deeper, will make their appearance later in the season—in the same spot!

1. Line the bottom of an outdoor pot with pea gravel; add 2 inches of potting soil. Plant daffodil bulbs.
2. Cover those with 2 inches more of potting soil; plant hyacinth bulbs.
3. Top with more soil; plant crocus bulbs. Add 2 inches of soil; water thoroughly.

IN-SEASON PICKS

FIGS If you've only tasted dried figs, the fresh kind will be a revelation—soft and sweet, with subtle crunch from the tiny edible seeds. Of hundreds of varieties, Black Mission and Calimyrna are the most common; when ripe, they should give a little when handled. Keep figs refrigerated, cushioning them with paper towels, and use within two (maybe three) days.

OKRA This Southern favorite is prized as a thickening ingredient in gumbo and on its own, coated in cornmeal and fried. Okra is also a staple of Indian-style curries. The slender pod should be smooth, with no soft spots or dry ends; use shorter pods (4 inches or less) when sautéing or frying; save longer ones for stewing. Store okra in a plastic bag in the refrigerator for two days—any longer and it can get slimy.

SWAP OUT SEASONAL ITEMS

Pave the way for crisp autumn days—and even cooler nights: Clear out hall closets to make room for heavier coats and jackets. Also, replace cotton sweaters and linen scarves with lighter-weight cashmeres and knits to carry you through the transition season, cleaning all items (and making any repairs) before storing them. Now is also a good time to clear out and donate anything you no longer wear.

Make your sofas and beds cozier with wool and fleece blankets and heavier, higher thread-count sheets. Air out any stored bedding on a sunny day to rid it of musty odors. Clean light-weight blankets and sheets, and store them for winter.

GENTLE REMINDERS

Take advantage of end-of-season sales at garden centers and nurseries. Skip annuals, as they won't come back next season; instead stock up on perennials and shrubs.

Start a meal-planning habit, now that summer has given way to the more bustling schedule of fall. Each weekend, plan menus, do your shopping, and get some prep out of the way.

Capture that late-summer tomato bounty: Spend a day making sauce, purée-ing them for soups, or slow-roasting and freezing them to enjoy throughout the winter.

Have a favorite apple variety? What's best at your local orchard will vary by the week, so give them a call or check their website before you go.

MARTHA MUST

It's important to rid the house of dust that collects over the summer, which is often full of allergy-inducing pollen. First vacuum woodwork and baseboards, using the brush attachment. Then wipe surfaces with a damp cloth and a mild cleaner.

READY THE KITCHEN FOR FALL

After a summer hiatus (of sorts), it's a joy to turn on the oven and prepare heartier meals using longer, slower methods. As you clear space and prep your kitchen for this heavy lifting, consider donating any unwanted (but still good) items to a local food bank or other organization.

Rotate the equipment: Put away the grilling supplies and ice cream maker, for example, and bring out the slow cooker, stockpots, and roasting pan.

Free up the freezer: Create room for big-batch sauces, casseroles, and soups to carry you through the season—and make weeknight meals more manageable.

Stock up on staples: Clear out any unused or expired pantry items and replenish cool-weather staples such as beans, grains, and broths, as well as baking basics for pie season (which kicks into high gear about now).

COOK

PREPARE A HEARTY SOUP

Follow this formula to make a big batch of simmering, satisfying soup:

1. In a stockpot, sauté aromatics (onion, celery, carrot); stir in some dried herbs.

2. Pour in enough liquid (water and/or stock) to cover; simmer 10 minutes.

3. Add quick-cooking vegetables (broccoli, cauliflower, green beans, peas, zucchini, corn), cut to uniform size.

4. Return to a boil, then reduce heat and simmer five minutes.

5. Stir in 1 cup cooked grains, pasta, or beans, plus 1 to 2 cups chopped sturdy greens (kale, Swiss chard, collards). Heat through. Serve with crusty bread or crostini.

UPDATE APPLE PIE

A few tweaks transform humble apple pie into a work of art.

Start by giving your pâte brisée an irresistible nuttiness: Replace 1/2 cup of all-purpose flour with 1/2 cup of nut "flour" made by processing nuts (hazelnuts, walnuts, or pecans) until finely ground; or simply use 1/2 cup of store-bought almond meal. Then fit the dough in a fluted tart pan with a removable bottom—it will yield a dessert with a sleeker profile that's easier to slice and serve than one baked in a standard pie plate.

For the filling, top homemade applesauce—spiked with Calvados, if desired, and given a blush of color from the apple skins—with concentric circles of petal-thin apple slices (easily done with a mandoline). Once out of the oven, brush with melted currant jelly for sheen—and a more rosy hue.

PLAN AHEAD FOR SCHOOL LUNCHES

The week's lunch-box menu is easier if you repurpose leftovers: Make meatloaf for dinner, doubling the recipe to get an extra loaf for using in sandwiches the next day—and even the next. Layer meatloaf slices on a whole-grain bun with toppings. Tuck in fruit and perhaps a cookie. Do the same for rice and beans (burritos!), grilled or poached chicken (avocado wraps!), or roasted vegetables (frittata!).

OCTOBER

It wouldn't be October without carved jack-o'-lanterns
and plenty of tricks and treats, but there are many other
reasons to love this harvest month—leaf-peeping
and -collecting among them. It's also when gardens are
put to bed and fireplaces are fully stocked.

SUNDAY	MONDAY	TUESDAY	WEDNESDAY	THURSDAY	FRIDAY	SATURDAY
				Have chimney inspected and cleaned; bring out all fireplace tools and accessories	Mow the lawn for the last time this season and clean up leaves	Celebrate Oktoberfest; invite friends over for craft beer and bratwurst
GARDEN Put fallen leaves to work (page 70)	Remove beach and picnic items from the trunk; vacuum interior thoroughly	Start (or join) a knitting or book club	Buy cough and cold medicines in preparation for winter	Clean gutters	Get seasonal flu shot	**GARDEN** **Sow seeds for spring vegetables** (in warmer regions) (page 70)
PETS Considering a pet? **Adopt a shelter dog**— or donate to your local animal rescue organization (page 71)	**COLUMBUS DAY** (Second Monday of October)	Clean and put away outdoor furniture	Move tropical plants indoors, if necessary	**HOME** **Order and stack firewood** (page 71)	Make Halloween costumes	Go leaf-peeping
KIDS **Craft Halloween decorations** (page 72)	Roast a big batch of brussels sprouts and other fall vegetables (and use in meals all week long)	Buy quince and bake into a pie or use in jellies and preserves	Take skis and other gear out of storage; buy replacements; register for ski passes	Put finishing touches on costumes and stock up on treats	Cut back perennials for winter	Visit a pumpkin patch and haunted corn maze
CELEBRATE **Carve pumpkins** (page 73)	Roast pumpkin seeds that you saved from carving pumpkins	Plant spring bulbs (up until December in southernmost states)	**KIDS** **Create leaf art** (page 73)	Clean and set up humidifiers	Bake and decorate spooky cookies (and make and freeze extra dough for the holidays)	**HALLOWEEN** (October 31) Go trick-or-treating!

GARDEN

PUT FALLEN LEAVES TO WORK

Once trees start dropping their fall foliage, don't just bag the leaves—they are among the richest organic matter around. Before raking, shred dry leaves by going over them with a mower a few times (use the "mulch" setting if your mower has one). Then you have options:

- Rake leaves into a pile or bin; let mature for at least a year into "leaf mold."
- Add shredded leaves to your regular compost (similar to grass clippings).
- Work the leaves into your soil; by spring, your garden will be all the riper for planting.
- Spread a 6-inch layer of leaves (as you would mulch) to protect plants from cold and wind (remove in spring).

GARDEN

SOW SEEDS FOR SPRING VEGETABLES

If you live where the ground is frozen fairly consistently throughout winter, you can pre-seed crops now for an early spring harvest.

- Start by digging in 2 to 3 inches of compost.

- Seed root vegetables (ones harvested in spring taste noticeably sweeter!), and brassicas a few weeks before cold weather hits to allow them to get growing.

- Wait to seed peas, spinach, and lettuces once the ground is too cold to germinate (so after the first frost).

- After seeding according to packet instructions, cover garden bed with a protective layer of mulch; cold frames and row covers also help (as does consistent snow cover).

ADOPT A SHELTER DOG

If you are looking for a new pet, consider giving a shelter dog or cat a forever home—thousands end up homeless each year. Buy bowls for food and water, as well as housebreaking pads, before you go, but wait to buy food, a crate and bed, and collars or harnesses until you know the animal's size and recent diet. Find a vet practice with experience treating rescue dogs—many shelters have relationships with vets and can refer you. Schedule that initial visit within two weeks of bringing your pet home, to be sure all vaccinations are current and get a baseline health exam.

ORDER AND STACK FIREWOOD

- When possible, ask to survey the wood before purchasing. Wood that has been aged (or dried) for six months to a year will burn more efficiently.

- Look for logs that are slightly cracked, with loose bark and a dull color.

- Choose hardwoods, such as oak and beech, which will burn slowly and give off more heat than softer varieties.

- Wood is often sold in quarter-split logs, by the cord; when stacked, it will measure four feet by four feet by eight feet long. Providers may stack for a fee, or you can do it yourself.

- On a level, dry base, stack two columns of wood at either end, Lincoln-log fashion; fill with remaining logs, stacked side by side in the same direction (front to back).

IN-SEASON PICKS

BRUSSELS SPROUTS Look for hard, bright-green sprout heads, with no mushy spots; those of roughly the same size will cook evenly. When possible, buy them still on the stalk, snapping them off before storing (the stalk absorbs valuable nutrients). Store brussels sprouts in a plastic bag in the refrigerator for three or four days, and trim stems before cooking.

QUINCE This centuries-old fruit cannot be eaten raw. When cooked, the rock-hard, sour white flesh turns soft, sweet, and deep pink. Choose solid fruit free of any wrinkling or bruising. Any fuzz will fall off as the fruit ripens. Keep in a bowl at room temperature until fully ripe (it will be golden and fragrant); for longer storage, refrigerate in an airtight bag for a month.

KIDS

CRAFT HALLOWEEN DECORATIONS

A ghostly gathering can haunt your house with this simple DIY.

1. Start with a plain sheet of white paper, and use a fringe cutter to cut strips along one long edge. (We used 8 ½-by-11-inch and 11-by-17-inch sheets.)

2. Fold the sheet over at every four-to-nine-strip interval, depending on desired width.

3. Use double-sided tape to secure ends, and scissors to round off the top edge for the ghost's head; use a black marker to draw on a face.

4. Open ghost into cylinder shape; tape a separate, 2-by-½-inch strip of paper inside the head to form a loop, then hang with clear monofilament. Repeat with different papers for ghosts in a range of sizes.

GENTLE REMINDERS

It's National Breast Cancer Awareness Month. Schedule your annual screening tests now. Check with the American Cancer Society (*cancer.org*) for guidelines.

If you live in an area with freezing winters, now is the time to have your sprinkler system professionally drained and serviced. Stake your lawn's boundaries, and flag any sprinkler heads near driveways and sidewalks, to prevent damage during snow removal.

Winterize your car: Apply wax to protect against salt; replace washer fluid with non-freezing formula; and swap out regular tires for winter tires, if needed in your area.

Trick-or-treat safety: Use reflective tape on kids' costumes and treat buckets to keep them visible to passing cars after dark.

CARVE PUMPKINS

With a basic carving technique, you can create classic jack-o'-lanterns or sophisticated patterns. For these daisy chains, do as follows:

1. Copy the template from page 279, then tape it onto the pumpkin. You can position it vertically or horizontally, so the stems snake either over or around the pumpkin. Poke holes along outline with an awl or T pin, every $1/8$ or $1/4$ inch. Remove template (keep nearby for reference).

2. Carve a hole in the back or bottom of the pumpkin (for lighting), then scoop out flesh, seeds (save these for roasting later), and pulp with a fleshing tool or plastic scraper.

3. Use linoleum cutters to scrape the pumpkin skin, working inward from the outline of the design. A No. 1 or 2 blade is best for details (3 or 5 for larger areas). Scrape in same direction so lines are unified. Use a drill to pierce flowers' centers.

4. Light the pumpkin with a candle or electric lights (the latter is safer).

CREATE LEAF ART

Gather fallen leaves, then turn them into silhouettes to display or share.

1. Trace a leaf onto watercolor paper with a pencil; gently erase so outline is barely visible.

2. Dip a paintbrush in water, then fill in leaf shape.

3. Working quickly, and with one color at a time, dip the brush in watercolor paint and very lightly dab it on the wet shape in a few spots—the paint will eventually spread and fill in the shape.

MARTHA MUST

Each season, I grow different varieties of winter squashes, such as butternut, acorn, spaghetti, and Japanese kabocha. Roasting is my favorite way to prepare them, cut into halves or wedges and enjoyed on their own, stuffed with grains or vegetables, or added to soups, salads, and pasta dishes.

NOVEMBER

As the start to the holiday season, November is when kitchens are cleared and then prepped for Thanksgiving and beyond. It's time to batten down the hatches, too—drafts sealed, boilers checked—in anticipation for houseguests and gatherings with good food and friends.

SUNDAY	MONDAY	TUESDAY	WEDNESDAY	THURSDAY	FRIDAY	SATURDAY
DAYLIGHT SAVINGS TIME ENDS (first Sunday of November) Set clocks back one hour	Pack away Halloween decorations	**ELECTION DAY*** Cast your ballot!	COOK **Make and freeze pie dough** or whole pies **(page 76)**	Dig up and store spring bulbs, especially dahlias and gladiolus	Plan Thanksgiving menu; make shopping lists; order turkey	Stock home bar for the holidays (buy wine by the case)
Test smoke and carbon mon-oxide alarms monthly. Change the batteries at least twice a year, or as needed	Check in with your local food bank about their needs for the coming season, and making a donation	Put out all bird feeders (and stop bringing them inside at night)	**VETERANS DAY** (November 11) Inspect trees for loose branches	Stock up on vitamin D supplements	HOME **Polish silverware** **(page 77)**	Organize baking spices and replenish as needed
Have ice skates and snow skis sharpened	Wrap boxwoods with burlap; layer compost over cut-back perennials	HOME **Assemble a winter car kit** **(page 77)**	Check house for drafts; seal with caulk or weather-stripping	Donate to coat drives	Treat winter footwear with waterproofing spray	Go on a sunrise hike or bike ride
Rub cutting boards with mineral oil to prevent from drying out; sharpen knives	Pick up turkey and other remaining items and ingredients	Choose Thanksgiving table settings	Prepare side dishes; bake pies; make centerpieces	**THANKSGIVING** KIDS **Make holiday crafts** **(page 78)** CELEBRATE **Send guests off with leftovers** **(page 79)**	Wash table linens	Play tag football with friends and family
CLEAN **Deep-clean the oven** **(page 79)**	Schedule holiday manicure/ pedicure and hair appoint-ments					

*ELECTION DAY Falls on the Tuesday following the first Monday in November, on or between November 2 and 8.

Feeling the winter blues? Vitamin D levels can drop with reduced sun exposure at this time of year, so consider asking your doctor about supplements.

The end of daylight savings time should be a reminder to do a safety check: Test smoke and CO alarms and replace the batteries. Check fire extinguisher pressure gauges, and stage a family fire drill.

Schedule a tree expert to come out and check for any branches that could damage your home or power lines on your property, and have them trimmed.

Prepare shoes and boots for slush and snow with a coat of spray-on protectant. If shoes are brand-new, apply two coats (wiping off excess and allowing them to dry in between).

COOK

MAKE AND FREEZE PIE DOUGH

For an unbeatable time-saver, make your favorite pie dough and freeze it right in the dish (up to three months), covered in plastic wrap and then in foil; thaw overnight before filling. Pecan pies and most double-crust pies—including the apple-pear pie and marionberry pie shown here—can be assembled and frozen (up to one month) before baking straight from the freezer. Pumpkin pies—and the sweet potato spin shown here—do not take well to freezing; bake those the night before but wait to top with meringue (and brown with a kitchen torch or under the broiler) the day of.

POLISH SILVERWARE

Polish your silver in November to use and display throughout the holiday season. Silver is easily scratched, even by paper towels or other silver pieces, so follow these tips from the experts:

■ To avoid fingerprints, wear white cotton gloves whenever dealing with silver.

■ Try washing lightly tarnished pieces with warm water and a gentle dishwashing liquid, then buff dry with a soft cloth, like flannel.

■ Use a store-bought polish (such as Wright's silver cream) for bigger jobs, rinsing and drying the pieces with a soft cloth.

■ If those steps fail to work, try buffing the silver gently with white vinegar.

ASSEMBLE A WINTER CAR KIT

Before you take off for the holiday, outfit your vehicle with a set of these emergency essentials.

Shovel, ice scraper, and sturdy brush: to help clear snow and ice on and around your car.

Spare hat, waterproof gloves, hand warmers, socks, and blanket: to keep warm in a pinch.

Phone charger: in case your phone battery gets low or dies.

Flares: to help you stay visible if you get stranded on a roadside.

Non-clumping cat litter: to help the car's drive wheels get traction.

Deicer: to thaw frozen door handles and wipers.

Jumper cables: to restart a dead battery.

Flashlight and extra batteries: to see and be seen in the dark.

IN-SEASON PICKS

BEETS Besides the familiar red variety, consider golden beets or pink striated Chioggias. When buying, look for beets that are dense and firm, with taut skin—and with crisp, dark greens attached. Once home, cut the greens to 1 inch; scrub the beets and refrigerate in a plastic bag for up to two weeks. Wash and refrigerate greens in a separate bag, wrapped in damp paper towels, for up to two days.

PERSIMMONS There are two commercial varieties: Hachiya and Fuyu. Look for smooth, firm, deep-colored fruit. Store Fuyus in a plastic bag in the refrigerator; they'll keep for up to a month. Hachiyas need a few days on your counter to soften up (next to bananas or apples for faster ripening); after that, refrigerate for two or three more weeks.

CREATE COLORING PLACEMATS

Keep children occupied until the meal is ready with a hands-on activity that doubles as décor. Ahead of time, sketch turkeys, leaves, and other appropriate shapes on brown or white kraft paper with a pencil—older kids can do this for themselves (or give little ones objects to trace). Set the sheets out with cups of crayons or washable markers and let the fun begin. In case any artists ask to take their handiwork home, you can roll the paper up and tie it loosely with twine.

MARTHA MUST

When handling a raw turkey, to keep the juices
from making a mess, I work on a large piece of parchment;
then I carefully crumple up the paper and discard it
and all the juices inside.

MAKE ACORN CRAFTS

For a fun Thanksgiving (or any day) activity, give kids a bunch of acorns in different sizes—or send them outdoors to gather their own. Then add "heads" to turn them into an acorn family. Mini acorns become babies, and bigger ones adults: Just pop off the caps (known as cupules) and glue them to wooden balls in corresponding sizes. Draw on facial features and hair with markers, then hot-glue the heads onto the nut "bodies."

SEND GUESTS OFF WITH LEFTOVERS

Thanksgiving is not just about gathering around the table for the main feast. Everybody looks forward to the leftovers, including your guests. Prepare ahead so you can send them off with care packages filled with all the fixings, such as in the nifty meal-in-a-box below—complete with a slice of pie. This will also lessen the load on your refrigerator while leaving plenty for your own next-day rummagings.

- Stock up on coated (so they're food-safe) kraft takeout boxes; the kind shown here can be found at many craft-supply stores and also online.

- Spoon cranberry, stuffing, and any other side dishes into small lidded jars or tins (or compostable "portion" paper cups, available in bulk online).

- Wrap moist foods such as sliced turkey and pumpkin pie in foil lined with parchment paper.

- Tuck in a few slices of toasted rustic bread so people can put it all (but the pie!) in a sandwich.

- Tie each box with colorful twine for a festive touch—and to help keep the flaps sealed tight during the drive home.

DEEP-CLEAN THE OVEN

Your oven works overtime during the holidays. Use this eco-friendly method to get it looking spotless.

1. Make a paste using three parts baking soda to one part each salt and water; three cups paste should do.

2. Remove oven racks and soak in warm soapy water; use paste on any tough spots (not on aluminum).

3. Fill openings with crumpled foil. Brush paste over interior, avoiding bare metal spots and oven door. Leave overnight.

4. Use a plastic scraper to remove the dried paste (wet the surface if needed), then wipe until clean with a damp cloth. Replace oven racks.

5. Clean grease from the oven door with a 50-50 solution of water and white vinegar, wiping with a soft cloth. Avoid wetting the gasket.

DECEMBER

Making merry is at the top of the end-of-year agenda, along with wreath making, tree trimming, cookie decorating, and open-house hosting. Planning (and crafting, buying, and even wrapping gifts) ahead means you can revel and rejoice— and ring in the New Year right.

SUNDAY	MONDAY	TUESDAY	WEDNESDAY	THURSDAY	FRIDAY	SATURDAY
		Plant indoor bulbs such as amaryllis and paperwhites for a lovely holiday display; put up Advent calendar for kids	Take holiday decorations out of storage; make any repairs	Craft ornaments and wreaths; make holiday cards; update mailing list	Prepare and freeze cookie doughs; mail holiday cards and gifts	Decorate exterior of house; string lights outside
Visit a tree farm to pick out an evergreen; trim the tree **GARDEN** **Keep your evergreen fresh** (page 82)	**CELEBRATE** **Deck the halls**; hang stockings (see page 82)	Finish shopping for and wrapping gifts	Plan holiday meals; make shopping lists; order specialty items	**HANUKKAH BEGINS AT SUNDOWN*** **CELEBRATE** **Make gifts from the kitchen** (page 83)	Plan holiday table settings	Hand out tips to service providers
WELLNESS **Do quick workouts** (page 83)	Stock up on spirits	**ENTERTAIN** **Prepare home for holiday houseguests** (page 84)	Take in a seasonal concert or performance	Organize kitchen tools; restock candle supply	**HANUKKAH ENDS AT SUNDOWN** **COOK** **Bake and decorate cookies** (page 84)	Host a holiday party or open house
Take houseguests (and dogs) on a long hike	**WINTER SOLSTICE*** Learn about rituals that honor the solstice	See a holiday light show (such as at a botanical garden) or drive around a festive neighborhood	Deliver gifts to coworkers, friends, and neighbors	**CHRISTMAS EVE** (December 24) Make eggnog; go caroling; set out cookies for Santa	**CHRISTMAS** (December 25) Celebrate with family and friends; recycle holiday paper	**KWANZAA BEGINS** (December 26) Take a welcome break by doing something you enjoy
Prune any damaged or broken tree branches outside	Wash table linens	Find a home for all holiday gifts (donate any you don't want or need)	**KIDS** **Create paper snowflakes** (page 85)	**NEW YEAR'S EVE** (December 31) Chill the sparkling wine (and add ruby pomegranate seeds to each glass)		

*__WINTER SOLSTICE__ Occurs sometime between December 20 and 23 in the northern hemisphere.

*__HANUKKAH__ Starts on the 25th day of the Hebrew month Kislev, which can occur any time from late November to late December.

KEEP YOUR EVERGREEN FRESH

A just-cut tree needs lots of water and some TLC to make it through the holidays. Here's what to do:

1. Before bringing your tree home, select a spot that's a safe distance away from heat sources such as a furnace, radiator, or fireplace.

2. Before putting the tree in its stand, saw off 1/2 inch from the bottom of the trunk (unless this was done for you when you bought it); this lets the tree soak up more water.

3. Check water levels daily (more often at the beginning) and replenish as needed—no additives necessary.

4. Limit how long string lights are left on; their heat dries out the branches.

CELEBRATE

DECK THE HALLS

You can gather boughs and trimmings right in your own backyard—or pick up some at a local nursery—to fill your home with seasonal finery. You'll find them in an array of evocative colors, textures, and scents (eucalyptus is an especially fragrant pick).

- Use evergreen branches and other foraged foliage—plus winterberries and pine cones—to make beautiful decorations, including garlands and the homemade wreath shown here.

- Fill hollow glass-ball ornaments (the kind with the removable metal caps) with small sprigs of holly, bayberry, and evergreens, leaving the cap off for 24 hours to prevent condensation from forming inside.

- Plant tender bulbs such as amaryllis, prechilled hyacinths, and paperwhites in attractive indoor pots and keep in a draft-free spot. Soon, you'll have a cheerful, mood-lifting display.

MAKE GIFTS FROM THE KITCHEN

Handmade treats are happily received—and they are great fun to make, too. Invite friends over and set up the supplies for cooking, baking, and packaging, assembly-line fashion.

- Start by raiding your canning collection—jams and pickles are always appreciated.

- Dried herbs are another great option. You can even create your own special blends (one for fish, another for pork).

- Put homemade granola in clear gift bags, seal with a sticker, and pack in a box—here a handsome compostable wooden one that's lined with colorful tissue—with honey or other favorite toppings. Wrap the box with waxed red-and-white twine.

- Or tweak the same packaging for cookies—easy to pull off with freeze-ahead doughs (page 84). Use cupcake liners or cellophane bags to separate cookies.

DO QUICK WORKOUTS

Amid the holiday crunch, it's more important than ever to keep energy up and stress levels down. The solution? Spend just four minutes each day on a Tabata workout. Do any exercise (jumping jacks, burpees, deep-knee lunges, push-ups) at maximum intensity for 20 seconds, rest for 10, then repeat, for eight rounds total. (As when starting any new type of exercise, don't overdo it, lest you injure yourself.)

IN-SEASON PICKS

PARSNIPS Early winter is the best time to find these root vegetables—after at least one hard frost, since the cold helps convert the starch to sugar. Commonly served boiled and mashed, they are even sweeter and more flavorful when roasted or sautéed in butter. Buy small or medium parsnips that are blemish-free; refrigerate in the vegetable drawer or a plastic bag for up to two weeks.

POMEGRANATES Red-purple in color, the pomegranate fruit husk has two parts: an outer, hard pericarp, and an inner, spongy mesocarp, which comprises the fruit's inner walls and seeds. When choosing pomegranates, look for fruits that are heavy for their size—a sign of juicy seeds inside. Mottled or darkened skin isn't necessarily bad, but the fruit should be firm to the touch. To remove the seeds, halve the fruit, hold one half cut side down over a bowl, and whack the back of the fruit with a wooden spoon.

PREPARE HOME FOR HOLIDAY HOUSEGUESTS

Create a warm welcome when hosting friends or family over the holidays.

- Dust and vacuum spare bedrooms thoroughly; change linens, providing extra blankets.

- Replenish toiletries and paper goods for the bathroom; clear space for guests' belongings.

- Make room in the entryway and/or coat closet for extra jackets; provide baskets or bins for hats and gloves, too.

- Stock up on snacks so guests can help themselves: mixed nuts, fruit, crackers, and assorted cheeses and dried sausages are all good options.

- Make a binder with instructions for electronics and entertainment (such as your Wi-Fi password).

COOK

BAKE AND DECORATE COOKIES

Before the holiday rush, make batches of doughs (here, sugar cookie and gingerbread) to keep in the freezer; roll them out and freeze on baking sheets, stacked with parchment and wrapped well in plastic (cut while still firm, the cookies will hold their shape beautifully). Then carve out a weekend for the whole family or a group of friends to do the decorating: Set out assorted cutters (or cut and bake cookies ahead of time) along with pastry bags or bottles with tinted icings, toothpicks (for drawing on details), and ribbon or twine for cookie ornaments, plus supplies for packaging as gifts (page 242).

CREATE PAPER SNOWFLAKES

Decorating for a New Year's Eve party is child's play when it involves cutting out these designs.

1. Start with a square of paper—wrapping paper, butcher paper, or text-weight paper (in different sizes for variety).

2. Fold paper in half diagonally to make a triangle, then fold triangle in half so pointed ends meet. Fold triangle in thirds, overlapping the left corner over the triangle; overlap the right-hand pointed corner over the triangle. Trim the pointed ends so base is straight.

3. Cut your folded paper with variations of cutouts; straight cuts are easier than curved. Unfold it gently. Don't worry if your snowflakes aren't exact: In nature, no two are ever alike.

GENTLE REMINDERS

Update your mailing list and begin writing holiday greeting cards early in the month—you should aim to mail them (as well as any gifts you're shipping) by the second week, to ensure on-time delivery.

Stock up on batteries in various sizes—especially if you have kids in the house, as their gifts often require them—and store them in a cool, dry place. Keep a small screwdriver on hand, too. And always include the necessary batteries with any gifts you give.

When you're entertaining, spills are inevitable—a little wine here, some melted candle wax there—so try to relax about them. Just keep stain fighters on hand, so you can tackle the spots after your guests go home.

Don't put the outdoor broom (or metal rake) away for the season. It's more useful than a shovel for removing snow from bushes, shrubs, and small trees.

PART TWO

ORGANIZE YOUR HOME

A home that's free of clutter conveys
a sense of calm and encourages productivity.
Use this room-by-room road map to help
guide you through your house. You'll find solutions
for putting the usual living spaces in order
and, where appropriate, methods for tackling
any problem spots—such as the kitchen
drawers and kids' craft tables.
Start by sizing up each area and taking
inventory of its contents so you know what
needs to go where. Then you can employ
the following strategies to make your spaces
more hardworking and rewarding.

ENTRYWAY

The entryway's primary purpose is a practical
one—and as a high-traffic, catchall area,
it has to work effectively. But there's no need
to surrender form for the sake of function.
As the first and last impression of your home,
the entry should be welcoming, too. Whether yours
is a generous foyer with a coat closet
or just a slim wall by the front door, some
clever tools and techniques will help you create
a space that satisfies on both counts.

Mounting knobs at a kid-friendly height will let little ones grab— and hang back up!— their own gear.

Use drawer pulls in assorted sizes to add pops of (custom) color, for DIY hangers.

An upholstered bench ups the comfort ante and provides a perch for you and your stuff.

A mesh bin keeps the small space airy and open.

EVALUATE THE SPACE

Before you delve into the organizing details, size up the situation. The below questions will help you decide what "entryway" means to you, and guide you in outfitting it for efficiency using the tips on the following pages.

DOES YOUR HOME HAVE A DEDICATED ENTRYWAY?

Even if you have a grand foyer, you'll want to incorporate ways to keep it from feeling cluttered. If not, work with what you have and get creative. Carve out an area near the main door, whether that's in a kitchen or hallway or living room. Or consider spreading out the components (storage bench, wall hooks, umbrella stand) over multiple walls and including the often-overlooked staircase wall.

WHO (BESIDES YOU) RESIDES IN THE HOME?

Certainly, the more people in the house, the more potential for chaos in the entry. Consider the needs of each person, including any little ones who need their stuff within reach. Is stroller parking a concern? Bikes? Pets that go outside count, too—you'll want to be prepared for muddy paws and leashes.

HOW OFTEN DO GUESTS STOP BY AND/OR STAY OVER?

Are you an avid dinner-party or weekend host with lots of guests traipsing in and out? Is your home the hub for the neighborhood kids? Besides members of the household, you'll want to make room for visitors, even if it's only on occasion.

HOW DO YOU TYPICALLY COME AND GO?

The single entryway of an apartment or small house will work a lot harder than that of a home with multiple access points. For example, some people mostly use the front door for retrieving the mail and receiving visitors, relying on the mudroom, garage, or kitchen route for lugging in the groceries and sports gear. How you use each space will determine what belongs where.

WHAT IS THE CLIMATE LIKE WHERE YOU LIVE?

If you have near-perpetual sunshine and moderate temperatures, your needs will be different (think sandy beach totes) from someone who lives where it's cold and rainy more often than not (requiring umbrellas and boot trays), or where snow and sleet (and parkas, scarves, hats, and gloves) are inevitable during the winter months.

WHAT IS YOUR BIGGEST ORGANIZING CHALLENGE?

Do you have to hunt down your keys every day? Maybe your kids tend to drop everything right where they took it off—creating a mountain of belongings by the door—or perhaps they hog the bathroom in the morning so you end up applying your lipstick just as you're dashing out. Even in our paperless, online-bill-paying society, the never-ending stream of mail can often be the biggest burden. Designated spaces and smart furnishing choices can address all your trouble areas. Be realistic and be prepared to embrace change.

PROJECT

COMMAND CENTER

Create a one-stop bulletin board—a store-bought cork board painted to complement the wall and outfitted with DIY details—to simplify the morning scramble.

1. Add a ledge (a strip of wood painted and mounted inside the board's frame) and curtain rod to corral the mail within plain sight—so nothing is forgotten.

2. Screw cup hooks into the ledge for keys; manila tags from an office supply store will help you keep track of whose keys are whose.

3. Tack invitations, lunch menus, and a monthly calendar—for at-a-glance reminders of appointments and events—to the board.

HALL CLOSET

A closet near the front door—even a relatively small one—is the holy grail of entryway organization. It makes it easy to control clutter and leave some space free for your guests' things as well. But there are even more ways to make the most of this behind-closed-doors space.

CURATE THE CONTENTS

A coat closet shouldn't be a shove-all. It's the most "public" of your closets, after all, and should be presentable. If yours has gotten out of hand, give it a thorough purge.

- Be realistic. Those items taking up valuable real estate on the top shelf? If they haven't been touched for six months or more, move them to longer-term storage or get rid of them. Even taking the items out and looking at them might inspire you to put them to good use.

- Reevaluate your system to determine what works and what doesn't. For instance, if your spouse has yet to ever place his jacket on a hanger, it might be time to assign him a coat hook. Ditto for the kids.

- Rotate the items by season. In spring, store away the winter coats and accessories, replacing them with raincoats, sun hats, and sunblock.

THINK VERTICALLY

Maximize your space's full potential— use top-to-bottom storage.

- Place baskets on the closet's highest shelf to gather up smaller items or those that see only occasional use, such as umbrellas and rain hats, and add a label or tag so everyone knows what's where; or use mesh baskets or wire bins to easily identify contents.

- Group hanging coats and jackets by wearer or by weight, using only sturdy wooden—never plastic or flimsy paper-covered wire—hangers.

- If space allows, put a multi-cubby storage unit (such as the stackable one shown opposite) down below for housing shoes, sorted by person or type; a unit like this also provides a low shelf for other items you need here, like a basket with the dog's leash and toys, and some old towels for drying off wet arrivals.

- Utilize door space: Add a basket per person for mail, if you don't have room in the entryway. Same for hanging a small mirror for last-minute touch-ups.

FAMILY-FRIENDLY CLOSET

Clever color-coding and intentional placements help this closet accommodate kids' and grown-ups' belongings alike.

1. Assign a color to hangers (using paint or ribbons) for each family member; same for baskets up top, which are striped with fabric paint (you could also use labels). Remember to leave room (and, if you like, designate a color) for visitors' gear.

2. Mount hooks at a height kids can reach for hanging jackets and backpacks; same for slim baskets that hold mittens and homework.

3. In lieu of wooden boot shapers, a simple binder clip at the top of rain boots will keep them standing upright; first let them dry outside the closet, on a boot tray or doormat.

MARTHA MUST

Always be sure to let wet coats, hats, and footwear dry outside the closet to avoid dirtying or dampening dry items. I have wall hooks and boot trays inside every entrance for this purpose.

KITCHEN

In an efficient kitchen, it's not just mealtimes that run more smoothly—it's your morning-to-night routine, from the first-brewed cup of coffee in the early hours to cleaning up after a dinner party. There are many simple and strategic ways to make the most of this bustling space: Keep frequently used items in the open and where they are used, group similar tools together, and employ storage containers and drawer dividers to customize all the spaces. These and other organizing principles will help you realize your kitchen's full potential.

A cabinet near the stove and sink puts dishes within reach when cooking—and makes it easy to put them away after cleaning.

Open shelves make good use of wall space above a sink, allowing you to keep a few favorite objects in the open but off of the counter.

Easy to maintain and stylish, Corian is an affordable alternative to granite for counters and islands. The wall shelves are in the same material for a cohesive look.

EVALUATE THE SPACE

Even the most spacious kitchen can feel short of room if it isn't organized thoughtfully. Begin, as always, by purging and sorting, so you are organizing only what you need.

TAKE INVENTORY

It's hard to get your kitchen in order if you don't know what you have.

- Begin by emptying out all the drawers and cabinets. This is a bigger job than you might realize, so try to find a free weekend to tackle the whole space at once. Have boxes on hand to hold everything while you sort.

- Empty one drawer or cabinet at a time, sorting like items into piles and getting rid of unneeded duplicates, broken or damaged items, or anything you haven't used in a while (unless it's part of a collection). Donate extras or store them in boxes for your next tag sale.

- Hold on to your prized collection of Japanese teapots or vintage pie plates, for example; as a beautiful display, they can make spending time in the kitchen more rewarding.

- Think about how—and how often—you use each of the items, so you can make sure to store them where you use them most. That means spatulas near the stove, knives and cutting boards near your work space, cups near the coffee maker, and so on. That also means keeping anything that you use only once or twice a year (like the heavy-duty turkey roaster) in the basement or garage.

- Before putting it all back, see if there are ways to expand the storage capacity of all the various cupboards and drawers, using the tips starting on page 104.

OPEN THINGS UP

When it comes to kitchen tools and equipment, seeing means using.

- Hang shelves over counters instead of cabinets for a lighter, more open space. Shelves make everything accessible for regular use.

- A combination of shelving and cabinets makes sense if you don't want everything on display—or if you rely on base cabinets under the counter to store items other than everyday dishware.

- You can also screw hooks underneath bottom shelves or upper cabinets for hanging items that would otherwise take up counter or drawer space.

- A hanging ceiling rack for pots and pans will save you valuable space down below. Put it over an island, if possible, or wherever you do the most work. Regularly using an exhaust fan while cooking will help to keep the hanging pots cleaner longer.

- There are also many ways to organize pots and pans and other cookware on the wall—either ready-made or DIY. Pegboard is a familiar option; it can be custom cut and painted to blend in.

FUNCTION AND BEAUTY

Maximize your kitchen's storage without sacrificing style.

1. Empty wall space is wasted space—even one (or three) small, strategically placed shelves will help free up counter space, such as for a few personal touches. This shelf houses an artful collection of vessels that is put into use when entertaining.

2. A freestanding wooden farm table adds warmth and work space (for a makeshift island), plus storage for baskets underneath.

3. Stowing dishwashing supplies in a stylish receptacle keeps the sink area tidy.

SINK AND COUNTER

Organizing strategies will differ depending on the particular spot or surface, and whether it's out in the open or behind closed doors (or drawers). Following are tips for tackling two of the most visible—and most used—areas of the kitchen.

TAME THE STUFF AROUND THE SINK

As arguably the busiest spot in the home, the sink and its surrounds should always be tidy.

■ Keep hand soap together with a nail brush (for those post-pie-dough sessions) in a soap dish—vintage ceramic ones are inexpensive and easy to find, or opt for sleeker, modern bamboo holders.

■ Put scrubbing and steel-wool pads in their own holder. These can end up with food bits trapped inside, so clean thoroughly; each time you make tea, for example, pour some of the boiling water over the pad to rinse it out.

■ Regular sponges also go in their own holders—be sure to rinse and squeeze well after each use. When they become too soiled for dishes after a couple weeks of frequent use, simply move them down below the sink for using on floors or other surfaces. Consider natural sponges, as they look lovely and last a long time. And note: the smaller the sponge, the less soap you'll use.

■ Stand bottle brushes, pot-and-pan scrubbers, and other such tools bristle-side up in a crock; remember what each is used for, or label them so others don't use the vegetable brush to wash a pot, and clean well after each use. If you don't use these regularly, tuck them under the sink.

■ Decant your favorite dishwashing liquid into a pretty reusable container. Buy soap in bulk to reduce cost and plastic waste.

■ Drying racks that fit neatly over the sink save space; when the basin is needed, rest the rack on a tray or mat on the counter.

■ Stack a bunch of terry-cloth bar towels, purchased in bulk, neatly near the sink for soaking up spills, wiping down counters, and drying off pots and pans.

■ To keep from rummaging around under the sink, install a sliding pull-out shelf or use a large lazy Susan, for easy access to your cleaning supplies; or corral these into separate, clear, stackable bins.

■ Suspend cleaning bottles by their spray triggers over a heavy-duty tension rod mounted across the under-sink cabinet; adhesive hooks inside the door can hold wet cleaning gloves and brushes.

KEEP COUNTERS CLEAR

More counter space often means more clutter. Make a habit of putting things away after every use.

■ Store essential tools within arm's reach of the stove, sorting them by usage (savory vs. baking) or material (wooden vs. metal) or category (spoons vs. whisks vs. tongs) into different crocks.

■ If you keep everyday appliances such as toaster ovens and coffee makers on the counter, use felt glides to protect the surface—they'll also be easy to slide back and forth.

■ Expand your work surface with a rolling cart for storage where you need it; this is especially useful in a tight kitchen. Add a custom-cut marble or butcher-block top, and a cart can also be used as a bar when entertaining.

■ Free up counter space by hanging knives from magnetic strips on the wall—or use drawer inserts (page 106).

(page 106).

MARTHA MUST

Don't wash your sponges in the dishwasher, as they really won't come clean. Instead, wash them in a mesh bag on a hot-water cycle in the washing machine with a couple of big towels. I also put my brushes and sponges outside in the sun once a week as a natural disinfectant.

KITCHEN ISLAND

Counters are one thing—a dedicated workstation is another, providing room for everything from prepping produce to rolling out doughs and even doing homework. In lieu of a permanent structure, you can repurpose all manner of tables or carts, finding a solution that fits your layout and lifestyle.

CHOOSE FOR USEFULNESS

More than just functional, an island is likely to become hang-out central. Take time when deciding on the right one.

- An island need not be grand to be helpful; a standard-sized one—typically four feet long and two-and-a-half feet wide—will provide plenty of work space.

- It also need not be custom-designed or even costly; sturdy stainless steel models in a variety of dimensions are available from restaurant-supply stores, while flea-market tables are ideal for using in this way.

- Unless the island is pushed against a wall, plan to have a clearance of two feet all around for navigating the usual tasks—and to allow room for helpers.

- Adding casters to the island's legs means you can roll it where it's needed—then tuck it away when not. Be sure to factor in the extra inches the wheels will add to the island's height. Or go with a small cart in a smaller space.

- If you plan to use the island as an occasional eating spot (or if it's your main dining area), having the top extend by about 6 inches provides space for tucking stools underneath; a clearance of 9 to 13 inches between the seat and the bottom of the counter allows for the perfect amount of legroom.

EXPAND THE STORAGE

Whether designing your own or retrofitting a repurposed piece, there are ways to make an island work harder.

- When possible, choose (or create) islands with open storage on the sides—it's an ideal spot to store oversize bowls and serving pieces, frequently used appliances, and favorite cookbooks.

- Group items on open shelves in attractive baskets and bins or atop trays, putting adhesive pads on the bottom of those so they slide out more easily.

- Mounted hooks or rods on the side of the island give purpose to unused space, putting tea towels where you want them.

MARTHA MUST

Install electrical outlets near the top of the island (or a counter or bar)—the more outlets, the better. This way you can use small appliances such as food processors and mixers where you need them most, and without the cords getting in the way.

EFFICIENCY BOOSTS

Big or small, kitchens can always be made more functional.

1. Two islands are better than one in a larger space, doubling the storage and work surfaces. Plus, you can designate one for the bulk of your prep work and the other for serving breakfast or brunch to a group of houseguests (or to double as homework central for the kids).

2. Hanging pots on a ceiling rack over the island means these tools are within reach—not taking up space in a cabinet. Or plan to store them on the island's shelves.

3. It's fine to keep out the items you use often or enjoy looking at—your prized mortar-and-pestle collection, for example, or bowls of fruits or vegetables. Just make sure there's ample room to do your work without always having to rearrange everything.

SHELVES AND CABINETS

Whether open, closed, or some combination thereof, these hardworking destinations tend to bear the brunt of kitchen storage. Optimize their capacity by rearranging dishware and putting even the between-spaces to work—always employing the guiding principle of kitchen organization: Keep things where you use them.

BE PRACTICAL WITH PLACEMENT

Storing things at the right height means they'll be easier to use—and put back.

- Keep the most frequently used items at eye level and within reach, whether on the lower shelf of an upper cabinet or a bottom open shelf, and in the most accessible location.

- Infrequently used items go on upper shelves; keep a step stool nearby to access those. Just avoid heavy and unwieldy things, as it can be tricky getting them down and back up again.

- Tongs are great for grabbing lightweight items—paper towels or boxes of cereal—on high shelves; hang a pair on a hook mounted inside the cabinet door.

- Heavy tools and equipment—mixers, slow cookers—should be kept below waist level, for easier lifting.

- Store cups and saucers the same way they're used: saucer, cup, saucer, cup. They'll not only look better, they can also be safely stacked higher—and are ready to go when you need a set.

CREATE MORE STORAGE

Try these tricks for getting cabinets and drawers to accommodate more.

- You can often add more shelves to existing cabinets (if you can't, try risers, as shown at right) or replace the shelves you have with pull-out models—especially in awkward, often space-wasting corner cabinets (lazy Susans also come in handy there).

- Install tension rods vertically between shelves, and use the space to stash cutting boards, sturdy platters, and baking sheets upright. Position the rods in front-and-back pairs, twisting to tighten and shifting them as needed.

- Divide drawers into smaller compartments, shopping at office-supply stores (think file or letter holders) in addition to housewares shops. Use organizers in different materials (plastic, bamboo, and metal mesh) to suit the contents; expandable ones are most convenient. See pages 106 to 107 for more ideas.

- Gain space by hanging stemware from racks mounted underneath a shelf or upper cabinet (or use the stemless variety); nest tumblers and juice glasses two deep.

- If there's a cabinet next to the oven, install hooks inside the door for holding oven mitts.

SPACE-SAVING CUPBOARDS

Closed cabinets are no excuse for being disorganized. This example shows just how much you can park behind a few cabinet doors.

1. Organizing items by color and use (so teapots and cups up top) also creates harmony and allows you to grab the whole set.

2. Adjust shelves to accommodate different items, grouping like with like—plates vs. glassware vs. deep pasta bowls.

3. Use risers and under-shelf units to double—or triple—the vertical storage, resting mugs atop plates, taller glasses over shorter ones.

THE DETAILS: DRAWERS

Already sources of easy-access storage, drawers can be made even more useful with some inexpensive dividers and smart sorting. Before you buy any organizers, it helps to empty out the drawers and sort like with like; you'll also want to measure inside drawers carefully, noting any hinges or other hardware.

PREP TOOLS

Combine your go-to knives and everyday utensils in a large drawer, separating them into right-sized bamboo (or other) boxes—juicers in one, graters in another—and lining them with cut-to-fit cork as desired for extra cushioning. Rather than getting a knife holder with presized slots, the flexible insert shown here has thin strips of soft cork that protect the blades and allow for different sizes. Either way, storing knives in a drawer instead of in the standard block frees up counter space (and you can add a safety lock to the drawer in case there are little ones running about).

FOOD STORAGE

It's worth investing in a matching set (or sets) of storage containers, preferably made of glass or BPA-free plastic; they will look so much tidier in and out of use (and they just might motivate you to make items ahead and be more intentional in creating and using leftovers). Nesting units like these take up less space; sort lids by type and size and stand them up in dividers. If space allows, keep water bottles and eco-friendly bags and wraps for packing lunches and other meals on the go.

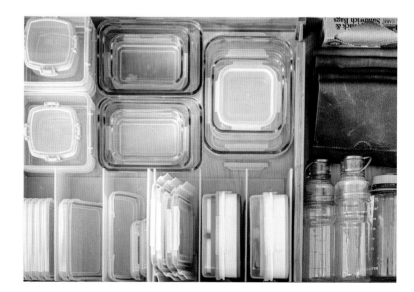

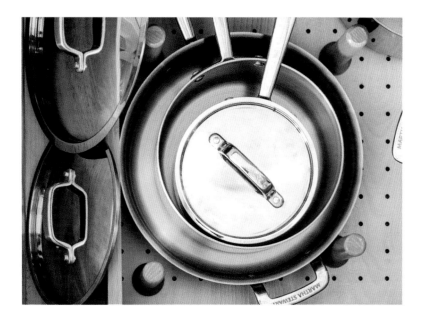

POTS AND PANS

A deep drawer is a convenient alternative to cabinets and/or shelves for holding pots and pans—just pull out the drawer to grab what you need (no more stretching or straining). Lining the bottom of the drawer with a pegboard insert (an option for some prefab drawers, or you can have it cut to size at a home-improvement store) lets you create custom spots for each pot or nested set, using pegs to keep the items in place. What's more, this setup can be adjusted over time to accommodate different cookware. Add a divider along one side of the drawer to stand up lids—and solve one of the kitchen's top organizing challenges.

JUNK DRAWER

Start by redefining "junk" to mean useful items such as home-office supplies and handy tools and hardware that don't belong anywhere else; then weed out anything you don't need or want (the true junk). Fit out the drawer with mesh bins in different sizes to house the sorted stuff; a lidded plastic bin with dividers keeps tiny odds and ends more orderly.

REFRIGERATOR AND FREEZER

Turns out, there is a right way to store perishables in the refrigerator and freezer for maximum shelf life. Just follow the tips below. And do a thorough cleaning of these units at least once a season, plus regular purging of leftovers and outdated items.

KEEP IT COLD

Most refrigerators have different temperature zones; be sure to check the owner's manual for specific guidance.

- The coldest spots are usually the bottom drawer and the back of the top or bottom shelf, closest to the vent, while the door will be the least cold (especially with frequent opening).

- Don't keep the door open longer than you have to—and be strategic when cooking, taking all your ingredients out of the refrigerator at once (rather than continually opening the door).

- Avoid overfilling the refrigerator, as this interferes with cold-air circulation.

- Tuck a baking soda box inside to combat odors, and replace it every month.

STORE IN THE RIGHT SPOT

Here's how to stock any unit for maximal use and optimal food safety.

- Always keep eggs in their original carton (to keep them from absorbing odors) on a higher shelf, where the temperature is most stable—not in the door.

- Store milk and other dairy products on the top shelf—preferably toward the rear, where it's coldest.

- Designate a middle shelf for leftovers, where they'll be most visible and likely to get eaten; use clear containers to see what's inside, and label and date as a reminder to you and others in the home.

- Fruits and vegetables can expedite one another's ripening and spoilage if stored in close quarters, so keep them in separate drawers (see right).

- The bottom drawer of the fridge—the coldest spot—is typically designated for meat. And keeping it there means it can't drip on anything stored underneath. If your model doesn't have that drawer, store raw meats on the lowest shelf, placing the package on a rimmed baking sheet in case of leaks.

- Keep cold cuts and cheese in a deli drawer, if your unit has one.

- Hold items with long shelf lives, including condiments and beverages, in the refrigerator door, where the temperature fluctuates the most.

ORGANIZE THE FREEZER

This food-storage workhorse has its own rhyme and reason.

- Divide the unit into zones depending on what you store there, but at least keeping sweets like ice cream separate from savory soups and casseroles.

- If your unit lacks compartments, use clear plastic bins to group like items.

- Keep foods in resealable freezer bags or clear airtight containers, noting the date and contents.

- Keep leftovers in the door if possible, where they are most visible.

FRESHER FRIDGE

Keeping fruits and vegetables at their prime is easier with these tips.

1. To ensure fruit gets eaten, make it accessible (here paired with yogurt for a grab-and-go snack).

2. Butternut and other winter squashes should be kept at room temperature until cut; after that, wrap them well in plastic and refrigerate on a shelf (not a drawer, where they may get overlooked).

3. If your refrigerator has a third produce drawer, keep leafy greens in the smallest one with the highest humidity. If not, wrap the greens in a damp paper towel and keep in a plastic bag in the regular vegetable crisper.

PANTRY

Maintaining an organized pantry saves you precious time. Employ a few basic strategies to help you do this: Sneak in storage, decant dry goods, and label everything. See page 215 for tips on what to stock in the pantry; having a good selection of items on hand also cuts down on meal prep time.

PURGE, THEN PLAN

Putting items in order will be easier when you start with a blank slate.

- When implementing (or revising) the pantry's organizing system, go through all your foodstuffs and toss out anything that's expired (page 112) or that you don't want or need. Do this at least once a year—such as in the weeks leading up to the holidays.

- Many items (basically all but meats, dairy, and fats) can be composted, or employ these no-waste options: Reassign expired baking soda to house-cleaning tasks; donate unexpired canned goods to a food bank; regift an unopened spice with a recipe to a friend.

- Before putting everything back, line the shelves with self-adhesive contact paper to protect against scratches and facilitate cleanup.

- Store small appliances in a way that makes it effortless to neatly lift them in and out.

DECANT DRY GOODS

This one simple step will save you space and create a cohesive look.

- For items you use a lot of, consider buying in bulk to save money—and reduce wasteful packaging. Whole grains and flours, dried pasta, and dried beans are all good options; be sure to shop from a store with high turnover to guarantee freshness. (Nuts and nut butters are other options.)

- Decant items into airtight containers or Mason jars. Label containers, and note any cooking instructions (such as for rice) inside the lid.

- When decanting items, it's also helpful to write the date you bought bulk food—or to note the best-by date from a package—on a small label on the storage container's bottom; this way you'll know when it's time to replace them.

- If there are pets in the home, you will save money by buying larger bags of food; store kibble in big bins that you can scoop right out of and keep treats in smaller containers on the same shelf.

GROUP LIKE WITH LIKE

How you define "like" here can vary—consider grouping by time of day, for instance, or by category.

- Divide the pantry into stations—baking supplies on one shelf, condiments on another, and pasta ingredients on yet another.

- Use removable labels or erasable chalkboard tags to identify each shelf section, letting everyone know where to put groceries away and find things when cooking.

- You can group similar products—oils and vinegars, for example—in individual trays, which will also help catch any drips. A lazy Susan serves the same purpose and allows you to see what's near the back of a deep shelf.

- Store kid-approved snacks at an accessible level, preferably in shatterproof containers; keep special "treats" on a higher shelf, out of eyesight (and reach).

- When storing cartons of broth or other products in their own packaging, put those with later best-by dates behind those that will expire sooner.

- If space allows, store extra paper towel rolls and other supplies here as well, on a higher shelf.

MARTHA MUST

Pinpoint the kinds of prep and cooking you do most often, and keep the ingredients you need for them in the same area. For example, I like to keep all the spices I use for baking, such as cinnamon and cardamom, in a tray that I can easily pull out when it's time to bake— especially during the holidays.

SPACE-SAVING PANTRY

A few tricks turn even small pantries into hardworking storage.

1. Pull-out shelves mean nothing gets lost in the back of the cabinet—and they easily replace existing stationary shelves.

2. Installing a magnetic surface—panels or strips—inside the door lets you keep tins of seasonings, sprinkles, and other small ingredients at eye level.

3. Stackable containers will maximize your space; clear ones make it easier to see what you're reaching for.

4. Potatoes and onions do best in a dark pantry or cupboard, so make room on a low shelf for these. Keep them separate, to prevent them hastening each other's spoilage, in open bins so air can circulate.

PANTRY STORAGE GUIDELINES

Shelf life depends on many factors: the type of food, the packaging, and the temperature at which items are stored. Below are basic storage guidelines; keep items at room temperature unless otherwise noted.

ITEM	SHELF LIFE	HOW-TO
Baking Powder	18 months unopened; 6 months opened	Keep in a dry place.
Baking Soda	2 years unopened; 6 months opened	Keep in a dry place.
Canned Goods	2 to 5 years; 12 to 18 months for acidic foods (tomatoes and fruit)	Keep in a cool, dry place; discard any cans that are bulging or badly dented.
Chocolate and Cocoa Powder	1 year	Keep in a cool, dry place.
Coconut (Grated)	6 months	Refrigerate after opening.
Cornstarch and Tapioca	2 years unopened; 1 year opened	Store in a cool, dry place.
Flour (White or Whole Wheat)	6 to 8 months	Store in an airtight container; freeze to extend shelf life (up to a year).
Gelatin (Powder)	18 months	Store in original container in a cool, dry place.
Maple Syrup	2 years unopened; up to 4 months opened	Refrigerate after opening.
Milk (Coconut, Condensed, or Evaporated)	1 year	Keep in a cool, dry place; refrigerate after opening, 1 week (coconut) to 2 weeks (condensed or evaporated).
Molasses	2 years unopened; 6 months opened	Refrigerate to extend shelf life.
Nuts	2 weeks	Freeze to extend shelf life; use within 6 months.

PERISHABLE GUIDELINES

As with pantry staples, foods that require refrigeration vary in how long they will last. Keeping them at a constant temperature (40°F) is key—return items to the refrigerator after using them, and store in the right place (page 108).

ITEM	SHELF LIFE	HOW-TO
Bacon	5 to 7 days	Freeze in resealable bag up to 1 month.
Butter	2 to 4 weeks in refrigerator	Freeze 6 to 9 months.
Cheese	2 to 4 weeks for soft cheeses; 2 to 4 months for hard cheeses	Wrap hard cheeses in parchment or cheese paper (not plastic wrap); these can also be frozen up to 1 year (do not freeze soft cheeses).
Eggs	2 to 3 weeks	Keep in original carton; do not store in the door.
Deli Meats, Turkey, Ham, Roast Beef	3 to 5 days	Freeze in resealable bags 1 to 2 months.
Fresh Beef, Lamb, and Pork	1 to 2 days for ground; 3 to 5 days for chops, steaks, and roasts	Keep meats in original packaging and place on a baking sheet in case of leaks; freeze ground meat up to 4 months; steaks, chops, and roasts, wrapped well in plastic, 6 to 9 months.
Fresh Fish and Seafood	2 days for fresh fish; 3 days for shrimp (peeled or unpeeled)	Freeze, tightly wrapped, up to 3 months for fillets, 6 months for shrimp.
Fresh Poultry	1 to 2 days	Wrap well in plastic and freeze parts (breast, thighs) up to 9 months, whole birds up to 1 year.
Fresh Sausage	1 to 2 days	Freeze, wrapped well in plastic, 2 to 3 months.
Milk and Nondairy Milks	10 to 14 days for dairy; 1 month for nondairy	Both types are best used within a week after opening.
Yogurt, Kefir, and Sour Cream	2 to 3 weeks before opening; 1 week after opening	Yogurt and kefir can be frozen for 2 to 3 months (do not freeze sour cream).

BATHROOM

Equal parts tidy and tranquil, clean and composed: Those are the promises of a well-considered bathroom. Yet organizing this vital space is an ongoing ordeal: Bottles and brushes and everyday basics must all coexist here. How to harmonize the hodgepodge and keep the personal effects under control? Take stock of what you have, reduce to the essentials, and make every inch count.

Potted plants liven bathrooms and purify the air—and thrive in the humid conditions.

A bath tray keeps soap and other toiletries where they are most needed.

Short on storage? Park a stool here and rest a basket on top, for spare towels and other supplies.

EVALUATE THE SPACE

For such a small space, a bathroom is required to hold a fair amount of stuff—often for multiple people and always with the goal of getting in and out with minimal stress. Before you can create the tranquil room of your dreams, you'll want to clear out the nonessentials and explore storage possibilities.

TAKE INVENTORY

It's easier to be organized when there are fewer items; start by purging.

- Toiletries have an expiration date so begin by tossing out anything that's past its prime; see page 120 for what to toss and when. (When purchasing new products, if there's no best-by date on the package, note the date of purchase on the bottom or on the decanted vessel.)

- The same goes for prescriptions and OTC items in the medicine cabinet—remove anything that's no longer needed or efficacious. Also, consider relocating these items to a small bin in the kitchen, which is most likely where you take them (and always keep these out of reach of children and pets).

- Cosmetics and hair products tend to pile up. Weed out duplicates or impulse purchases—anything you are not using regularly should go. Give costly or quality items to others; many unopened products can be donated.

- It helps to keep a few cleaning supplies here (for routine spot checks), but store the bulk of these in an out-of-the-way location, such as a linen closet.

- Keep only a month's worth of toilet paper in an under-sink cabinet or in a basket or bin—leaving a few rolls near the toilet for easy access—and stash the rest someplace else.

MAKE EVERY INCH COUNT

Even spacious bathrooms often lack sufficient surfaces and hiding spots. Here are tips for solving that dilemma.

- When buying or designing new sink cabinetry, look for a model that offers different compartments (drawers or cubbies)—preferably one for each person who shares the space.

- Central bathroom cabinets can be fitted with roll-out wire trays (the kind used in kitchens). Keep a first-aid kit and miscellaneous toiletries on them, or even the trash can.

- Pedestal sinks pose their own storage challenges, since they lack cabinetry and counter space. This is when shelves or furniture can come to the rescue. An above-sink medicine cabinet will also help, if that fits into your design scheme; otherwise, get creative with using floor space, such as with attractive bins and baskets.

- Floating or bracketed shelves make excellent use of wall space. If your shelves are over the tub, consider using metal (hotel) models that allow the air to circulate and keep the contents dry.

- Towel rods are another way to put walls to work—you can even mount several on the back of the door, leaving room for a draped towel between each (or see page 118 for another door idea).

see page 120 for what to toss; page 118 for another door idea

SERENE BY DESIGN

Take lessons from your favorite spa to turn your own bathroom into a private retreat.

- Cut the clutter and create a relaxing environment by keeping all but the everyday essentials tucked away and out of sight.

- If your bathroom is short on storage, get creative: Stack hand towels in a wicker basket next to the sink; keep soap and other items on a tray on the counter or nearby shelf; use a bathtub tray to hold the accoutrements of a hot soak.

- Place an ottoman (or stool or chair) by the tub to hold reading material or spare towels.

- Swap out your regular towels for Turkish textiles—they air out more quickly, avoiding the need for frequent washings (and they become even softer and more absorbent over time).

STRATEGIZE THE STORAGE

Now that you've pared down your provisions, you'll want to give all the keepers a logical home. Let your usual routine—and any space constraints—help dictate what goes where. The following solutions target the typical problem spots.

STREAMLINE CABINETS AND DRAWERS

Ease the morning shuffle by designating a place for everything—and being mindful of always returning items to their rightful spots.

- Gather myriad toiletries into upcycled jars and vases. Borrow vessels from the kitchen or garden.

- Containers, baskets, or drawer dividers can give order to makeup items: mascaras in one, lipsticks in another, brushes and applicators in another still.

- Keep hair accessories, like hair ties, in a small container together with a brush.

- Transfer cotton swabs and balls from their original packaging into attractive vessels.

- Place your frequently used products on shelves within arm's reach, and keep kids' supplies at their level.

- Lazy Susans help to extend your reach when storing products on deep or high shelves.

- Ideally, store a hair dryer in a drawer outfitted with an outlet. Or fasten a pair of hooks inside an under-sink cabinet door—or in a convenient place on a wall that's near an outlet.

- Stash your everyday cosmetics in a pouch that's pretty enough to keep on a shelf yet portable for when you need to carry it to another room or out the door.

KEEP SINKS AND TUBS IN CHECK

It's all too easy to let these areas get overcrowded, especially when there's a lack of other surfaces (hint: add shelves).

- Store toothbrushes in holders—one for each person; if counter space is tight, mount a small shelf near the sink (or use suction holders).

- Add corner shelves in a shower to hold shampoos and such—or hang a stainless-steel caddy over the shower-head.

- Bathtub trays are especially helpful for clawfoot tubs, which typically have no ledge or flat surface for products.

- Rather than keep a whole bar of soap (which is slippery when wet and leaves hard-to-clean residue on its holder), shave off shards and insert into the center of a natural sea sponge (use a utility knife to slice into the center).

- Decant shampoo, conditioner, and body wash (buying them in bulk saves money) into pretty nonbreakable bottles, adding labels for easy identification.

- Keep only one bath towel out for each person at a time and store the rest, ideally in a linen closet or laundry room to keep kids from grabbing a new one each time. Extra washcloths and hand towels can go near the sink—out of the way but accessible.

SPICE-RACK SOLUTION

Lightweight and unobtrusive, these simple kitchen racks come ready to hang—perfect for a back-of-the-door station.

1. Stand combs, your most-used makeup brushes, and everyday cosmetics in sturdy glasses so you can see them at a glance and grab them quickly.

2. Include a mirror for applying makeup. Set it in a secure stand, like this one, or use adhesive strips to attach it to the door, so it doesn't topple.

3. Put items you use in tandem, like facial cleansers, treatments, and cotton pads, on the same shelf to streamline your routine.

4. Invert the lowest rack for a towel bar and accessories perch; just slip out the two keyhole-shaped brackets on the back, then flip before popping the brackets back in and hanging the rack upside-down.

COSMETICS STORAGE GUIDELINES

All cosmetics have a limited shelf life, so be sure to weed out expired items
as part of your organizing routine. Going forward, do this exercise at least twice yearly,
such as when transitioning from one season to the next. Monthly is even better.

ITEM	LASTS	TOSS SOONER IF
Moisturizer: Face or Body	About 2 years in a pot; 2 to 3 years in a pump	You notice a change in the smell or consistency.
Liquid Foundation, BB Cream, Tinted Moisturizer	Up to 2 years	The color changes or separation occurs.
Makeup Brush	Indefinitely with routine cleaning	The bristles start to snap or shed.
Powder: Eye Shadow, Blush, Face Powder	Up to 2 years	It gets suspiciously crumbly or shiny (a sign that it has attracted moisture—a breeding ground for bacteria).
Mascara, Liquid Liner	3 to 4 months	You get an infection, such as pink eye, or it dries out (bacteria gets transferred easily from eyes into container via the brush).
Lipstick, Lip Gloss, Lip Balm	1 year with wand, 2 years with direct or brush application	If you get a cold sore or any infection on or near your mouth, ditch all lip products and replace.
Eye and Lip Pencils	Up to 3 years, with sharpening	It becomes either unusually dry or melty.
Sunscreen, Sunblock	Up to 1 year	The expiration date on the tube or package has passed.
Nail Polish	Up to 2 years if opened (indefinitely if not)	It thickens and/or separates.
Electronic Face Brush	Up to 3 months, for the brush head	The bristles becomes distressed and bent out of shape.
Loofah	About 2 months; longer if not used very often	It begins to discolor.
Hairbrush	Indefinitely	The bristles are bent or falling out.

Moisturizers with a pump dispenser minimize bacteria and optimize shelf life. If your favorite comes in a pot, use a spatula instead of your fingers to apply. Also note: Organic and natural creams and lotions may last longer when kept in the refrigerator.

Even the bit of oxygen that seeps into foundation when you open and close it can cause the product to break down faster. Cap bottles tightly after use—or choose one with a pump dispenser.

Swirl brush heads on a bar of facial soap to loosen debris. Then rinse the bristles thoroughly with warm water. Repeat these steps until the water runs clear. Let brushes dry overnight on a towel, making sure the heads hang over an edge to keep their shape intact.

Apply eye shadow with your fingertips, tapping (not rubbing) over the lid—or use your foundation as eye shadow.

Prevent under-eye smudging by applying clear brow gel over mascara after it dries—and use the brow gel to tame any flyaways around your face, too.

Glosses with application wands are prone to introducing bacteria into the tube. To keep it cleaner, swap the wand for a washable brush.

Sharpen often to get rid of the part that touched your face, where bacteria lives.

Sunscreens and sunblocks usually come stamped with a use-by date. But because their active ingredients break down over time, always toss them within a year of opening, to be on the safe side.

To thin the polish and make it last longer, add a few drops of nail-lacquer thinner.

Dislodge particles from the brush head by rubbing it against a dry washcloth. Every few days, apply a non-soap wash to the device and turn it on to work in the cleanser. Then rinse it with warm water and let it air-dry.

Before sudsing up, run your sponge under hot water and rub body wash or soap into it. After bathing, rinse it well with hot water again and dry it outside the tub by hanging it on a hook or cabinet handle.

Remove loose strands after each use by running another hairbrush through the bristles. (Or do as Martha does: Lift away mats with an orange stick.) To cut through dirt, deep-clean it every few weeks by soaking the brush in one part apple-cider vinegar to two parts warm water. Then rinse it with warm water for a few minutes and let it dry overnight.

LIVING ROOM

Conversation hub, entertainment center, fireside retreat—the living room is all that. As the spot where guests tend to congregate, this space should also be conducive to lingering and lounging—and feature your personality and style. Keeping surfaces curated is the organizing goal. Make it happen by giving everything a home.

Placing a mirror on the wall behind a sofa opens up a small living room; the brass frame adds warmth to the otherwise neutral palette.

A wall-mounted lamp such as this industrial-style model is an up-to-date alternative to a floor lamp—and avoids the need for a side table.

Group smaller objects on a tray to keep the table clutter-free (and easier to clean).

With (almost) nothing interrupting the sight line, this timeless coffee table makes the space appear bigger.

EVALUATE THE SPACE

A living room should invite intimate chats, while still allowing for easy flow when entertaining. Whether you are embarking on a total redo or simply implementing a few tweaks, try these tips for creating a space that best satisfies your situation and style preferences.

DEFINE THE PURPOSE

The first step is to figure out the role of your living room, as it can differ in every home and even over time.

- If it doubles as a den, you'll need to contend with the TV (see right)—and provide ample seating for comfy viewing.

- When part of a great room, it helps to section the space into activity zones—one for conversation, another for playing games, yet another for casual meals.

- To delineate a living "room" in an open floor plan, partition it off from the other areas by placing the sofa with its back to the dining table, or by using an open bookshelf or other room divider.

- For frequent entertaining, consider creating two separate hubs by orienting chairs and/or sofas around an accent table, each group anchored by an area rug.

- Bay windows or cozy corners with views are ideal places to park a pair of padded chairs next to a floor or table lamp, for a reading nook.

PROVIDE A FOCAL POINT

Be intentional about giving your eye a pleasant landing spot. While this design principle is true for all rooms, it is especially so in this gathering place.

- A focal point can be structural, such as a fireplace or a picture window, or constructed—a striking piece of artwork, for example, or a gallery wall.

- While it's nice for the main perch (usually the sofa) to have an ideal view, that's sometimes not the case. Better to have the view framed by the entrance.

- Color, too, can draw the eye, such as by painting a wall—or the inside of an imposing china cabinet or bookcase—in a bold shade, or using a patterned wallpaper to create a similar effect.

ARRANGE THE FURNITURE

It's important to work with your room's layout when positioning the pieces.

- Avoid clogging up the entrance to the living room with a sofa or potted plant; keep this area open and therefore more welcoming.

- In general, there should be two feet around all furniture and other items in a living room, for good traffic flow.

- When possible, aim to have at least 18 inches between a sofa and chairs, so people don't feel too hemmed in. You can always move the furniture closer when entertaining to allow for quiet conversation and make room for pathways.

- In long, narrow living rooms, the challenge is to leave at least 14 inches between the sofa and coffee table. Using a pair of smaller tables allows you to move one elsewhere when guests drop by.

MANAGED MEDIA

Smart TVs and other devices allow for endless streaming, but at a cost—a big blank screen (and all those unsightly cords).

- Conceal the TV in an armoire, integrate it into a built-in (as on page 129), or hide it behind custom shutters mounted on either side or a roller blind hung from above.

- To contain wires, use fabric sleeves (meant for pendants) or wall-mounted cord-cover strips; a rotating power strip tucks away neatly.

- Store remote controls on their own tray or in a pretty box. Flatware caddies and desktop organizers have compartments to stand the remotes upright.

SEATING AND ACCENT TABLES

An organized living room begins with the major furnishings—seating, tables, lighting—and is enhanced by well-chosen accessories. Odds are, you can rethink and reposition a lot of what you have, but a few upgrades might ease the way.

SCALE IT RIGHT

Getting a right-sized sofa is critical for comfort. First things first—measure, twice.

- In general, aim to have 14 to 18 inches of wall space on either side of a sofa, whether or not side tables will be going there. The exception is for sectionals, which often snuggle up against adjacent walls.

- Too-big furniture can overwhelm a room and block traffic. Too-little pieces can be just as problematic—and you'll end up with lots of awkward, open floor space.

- Settees and sofettes and "apartment" models look smart without eating up a lot of square footage. Those with lots of air underneath also keep the room light on its feet.

- Avoid overloading the sofa with throw pillows; two to five is a good range, mixing as desired.

- In especially tight areas, forgo a sofa and group four chairs around a coffee table instead (again using a rug to pull them together).

- Poufs and ottomans offer seating and surface—and even storage—in one stylish package (see page 131 for one idea).

- Floor pillows are nice to have for casual group hangouts, and they stack neatly when not in use.

CLEAR THE DECKS

Resist the urge to let stuff pile up on every surface.

- Spend a few minutes at the beginning or end of each day clearing away what doesn't belong from coffee and end tables.

- A coffee table with a lower ledge doubles the surface area; same for two-tiered end tables—or use nesting tables for as-you-need-it convenience.

- No ledge? Stow handsome baskets or bins underneath tables for housing items you don't want on display (e.g., remote controls).

- A vintage chest is a good coffee table option for stashing a collection of games or extra throws.

- To give accent tables a unified look, set out attractive trays to hold smaller trinkets and vessels.

- Coffee table books are meant for these surfaces; just be sure to stack them neatly and not too high.

- Keep a catchall basket for all the ephemera that accumulates in this shared space—and put away the items once a week.

MARTHA MUST

I make a point of measuring all my rooms, noting the door and window placements. Then I print out each room on card stock, laminate the cards, and punch a hole in the top for stringing on a key ring to use in future decorating jobs.

SOFA SMARTS

This piece alone can make a room; here's how to ensure yours is up to the task.

- When buying a new model, look for the best-quality one within your budget; major discounts usually kick in over President's Day and summer holidays.

- Try to actually sit on a sofa before buying, to find out if it's comfortable for you.

- Think about your lifestyle: If you have kids and pets, you may not want a light-colored sofa or one made of hard-to-clean fabric.

- Sleek, single-seat cushions (aka bench seats) can sink in the middle over time; choose one that flips and anchors to the sides with hooks.

BOOKCASES AND SHELVES

Whether you go for custom built-ins, freestanding bookcases, or mounted shelves, these storage stalwarts put wall space to work and free up other surfaces. Use one or a combination for an ultra-organized space.

GO VERTICAL

Stacking books on the floor or atop furniture is certainly one way to store them; here are other, more orderly options that will keep your volumes—and your living room—in pristine condition.

- Built-ins offer space-saving storage and seamless design, and are especially useful at flanking a fireplace or camouflaging your TV and consoles (see page 124 for ways to manage the media). They're also worth the investment for anyone with a sizable collection of books.

- If built-ins aren't an option, you can achieve a similar look with freestanding or wall-mounted shelves, particularly if you cover an entire wall and add trim pieces painted to match.

- Having floor-to-ceiling cubbies or shelves creates the biggest impact and provides the greatest storage; being able to customize the configuration over time means you can accommodate different items at various stages of your life and as your interests wax and wane.

- To showcase volumes with striking covers—say, books on architecture, photography, travel, and/or art—you could create a gallery wall by mounting floating ledges and resting the books on top, covers facing out.

CURATE THE CUBBIES

Organize books and objects like you would anything else: Start by winnowing your collection to what you want on display (store the rest elsewhere, or donate), then plot out an arrangement. As you place items on shelves, step back now and then and reposition them until you find a look you like.

- Unless it's a library look you're after, it's better not to cram books in all cubbies, or even end-to-end on an entire bookshelf. Besides being more appealing to the eye, leaving some open space will make cleaning the surfaces, and taking down and putting up favorite reads, so much easier to do.

- Arrange the books in a way that looks good and makes sense to you—whether that's alphabetical by author, by subject, or by color, width, or height—or even just randomly.

- Accessorize the shelves by incorporating ceramics, sculptural objects, framed photos, collectibles, even houseplants— pretty much anything you admire and that enhances the overall effect.

- If the unit will double as entertainment center, carve out one shelf at eye level for the TV; you can even tuck a small speaker in one cubby or on a shelf without it announcing itself, then hide unsightly routers and other devices in closed cabinets down below (if shelves are mounted to the wall, station a media console beneath to stash it all).

DISPLAY 101

The most visually pleasing bookshelves wed practical storage with individual style.

1. Stack some books horizontally to break up the pattern—and to bookend upright volumes. Rest small decorative items atop some of the stacks.

2. Don't be afraid to inject some whimsy into the mix with unexpected pieces, such as this "ancient" statue-cum-vase.

3. Establishing a theme helps to unify the decorative objects, here animals and other nods to adventure collected from the family's travels.

4. A quick way to "hide" the TV when unexpected guests stop by is to use the wallpaper feature: Look for a model that lets you display images when it is on low-power mode (use this feature only when people are around, to conserve energy).

THE DETAILS: FINISHING TOUCHES

Each of the following provides a solution for common living-room conundrums: what to do with a mishmash of media devices; where (and why) to set up a home bar; and how to finesse the fireplace mantel. Plus, when sneaking in storage, why a custom ottoman just might be the answer.

MEDIA CENTER

When shopping for ways to house your sound system or streaming devices, look beyond furniture pieces specifically designated for that purpose. Here a cabinet with sliding doors and adjustable inner shelves does the job beautifully. Putting a wood slab on top (have one custom-cut at a local lumber yard or home-improvement center) gives it living-room cred. Besides providing a surface for displaying art, coffee table books, and potted plants, the credenza is also the perfect spot for a TV (and remote controls can be kept behind closed doors).

BAR CART

The living room will be instantly more convivial when appointed with a drinks station. A rolling cart is a classic choice, capable of being wheeled to wherever the party is—and looks lovely the rest of the time, taking up minimal space against a wall. For a similar stationary option, repurpose a credenza or armoire (such as the one on page 230). When the elements are in the open, as here, you'll want to keep them orderly. Use trays for holding bottles, bar tools, glassware, and ephemera such as plants; touches of brass lend swankiness to the collection.

MANTEL DISPLAY

The mantel is often the focal point of the living room, so it's worth being intentional in arranging what goes there. Start by including items of varying heights. Here this is achieved not only with the items resting atop the mantel—slender taper candles, two different-size vases (one cylindrical, the other more organic), and a spherical match holder—but also with hung mirrors, which meld into the arrangement. There's also nothing inherently wrong with a symmetrical arrangement, but grouping items together to one side (as shown) or having each side be different, can look more natural, less rigid.

OTTOMAN PLUS

Not all living rooms can accommodate a coffee table, bookshelf, and extra seating. That's what inspired this multi-purpose ottoman, made of three basic elements: a quartet of unfinished wood boxes (sold at crafts stores or online), screwed together in the configuration shown; a cushion on top (this tufted marigold version is held in place with Velcro fasteners), and casters underneath for easy maneuverability. Leave the cubbies unpainted for a Scandinavian look, or paint them—here with a base coat of white and a stenciled geometric design.

BEDROOM

It's where you greet each new day,
prepare for your busy life, and unwind each
evening. As such, there's great value in
keeping the bedroom in good order, with
everything in its place and nothing to impede
a fresh start or a restful night's sleep
(see page 135 for more ways to boost your
beauty rest). Equally important: This
is your sanctuary, so fill this space with things
that make you happy, just because.

A headboard isn't strictly necessary, but having one helps to define the bed and the overall look of the room.

Keeping plants in the bedroom has been shown to purify air and improve sleep. Plus, nature is the best decoration.

Lightweight layers allow you to shed them during the night, when body temperatures naturally rise.

EVALUATE THE SPACE

Bedrooms come in many sizes and configurations—but they all should be sanctuaries of sleep. Paring down is a first step to keeping your personal space more tranquil; troubleshooting with smart and stylish storage is the next.

STRIVE FOR SERENITY

Keep the bedroom's primary purpose front and center when organizing it.

- With your head propped on a pillow, take in the view from your bed. Is there anything that interferes with your peace and enjoyment? If so, move it elsewhere.

- Also picture what you'd like to see from this perspective, such as a view outside a window, inspiring artwork, or a favorite collection—even houseplants.

- Keep the bed itself free and clear of anything other than bedding and throws.

- Curate the nightstand to hold only items that provide comfort and create bliss (see page 136 for more tips).

REFINE THE SPACE

Besides a sleep sanctuary, ask yourself what else you'd like your bedroom to be.

- Do you long to have a reading nook (even a cozy chair) or a quiet place to meditate? Think of ways to arrange the furniture to make that happen, even if that means forgoing a dresser.

- Is a TV really necessary here? It takes up space that could go to something else—and is a sure invitation to binge-watch until the wee hours.

- If the bedroom must share space with the home office, look for ways to hide the work when you're done. A secretary or converted armoire looks lovely when closed. Or keep only personal and decorative objects in plain sight on a desk.

TAKE INVENTORY

Devote due time to edit your wardrobe at least twice each year, preferably with someone whose opinion you trust.

- Working with one drawer or category at a time, comb through every item of clothing and all the accessories.

- Then donate, gift, or sell anything you haven't worn in the past year (and likely never will) or that no longer fits. Toss anything that's beyond repair.

- Lastly, sort the keepers into categories so you know what will need to go where.

EXPAND THE STORAGE

Clutter has no business here. Use stylish solutions to achieve a sense of calm.

- Underbed bins and baskets can be used for storing extra bedding, shoes, or scarves (but nothing from other areas).

- A bench or chest at the foot of the bed offers a place to sit while getting dressed and to store spare blankets.

- For a hardworking headboard, find one with a built-in bookcase (see opposite), which puts space behind a bed to good use (in place of bedside tables).

- Shelves next to or above the bed also replace the need for nightstands.

- Dressers or writing desks make excellent use of bedside square footage.

- Wall hooks and rails let you hang scarves, sweaters, bags—even jewelry.

EVERYDAY UPKEEP

Here are three steps to keeping a tidy and tranquil bedroom.

- Make the bed first thing every morning, before you even leave the room.

- Put away clothes as soon as you take them off—either back in the closet or dresser or, for dirty clothes, in the hamper. (And picking out your outfit the night before will give you time to put back any rejects.)

- Don't leave shoes lying around on the floor, either; these tripping hazards should go where they belong—or at least in a designated bin inside the room.

BED AND NIGHTSTAND

A bedroom's calm is all too easily breached by tossed-aside clothes and teetering piles of reading material. It's also easy to shortchange this private retreat in the style department—yet delighting in the décor will definitely improve your mood.

BETTER THE BED

Your bed is the most important piece of furniture in your room—and where you spend roughly one-third of your life. Be pragmatic but also a bit indulgent.

- Prolong the life of your sheets by alternating sets with every washing; this will also allow you to make your bed while you're doing the laundry.

- Use protectors to extend the life of your pillows and mattresses—hypoallergenic ones will further shield them from dust mites and pet dander, among other triggers. Waterproof covers are a must in kids' rooms.

- Even with protectors, you'll need to replace old pillows if they no longer pop back into shape when folded over.

- Threadbare comforters are not just eyesores—they won't do their job of keeping you warm at night (or protecting the down inserts, if it's a duvet cover). Swap them out for fresh ones.

- To keep your comforter from shifting inside the cover, try this trick: Turn the cover inside out and sew two pieces of fabric tape to all four corners. Then tie the fabric tape around each corner of the comforter and turn right-side out.

- Reversible duvet covers or bed-spreads let you freshen up your room on a whim—bonus points for those where both patterns are visible when it's folded back.

- Use decorative pillows and throws to layer on the comfort—but don't overdo it, since they'll add to the bed-making.

- Park a bench or chest at the foot of the bed to house the extras during the night (not on the floor). Stack blankets on a wooden chair, where they won't be forgotten. Just be sure these pieces don't get buried under piles of clothing.

NEATEN THE NIGHTSTAND

Be intentional about these sidekicks—they play a supporting role in ensuring a good night's sleep (see right for more).

- Chairs and stools, vintage ladders, even desks and dressers are all appro-priate stand-ins for the standard bed-side table. Choose the one that provides the amount of storage you need.

- A floating shelf or cubby leaves the area underneath open for other storage or just keeps the space airy and light.

- In lieu of a table lamp, sconces or pen-dants free up surface area on the night-stand—or use an elegant floor lamp.

- Cords and chargers do not make for a restful environment; better to tuck these in a drawer or hide them in a bin.

- Make use of bedside pouches or "caddies" (sold online and at house-ware stores) that tuck between the mattress and bed frame for holding reading materials.

NIGHTTIME NECESSITIES

Bedside tables are easy to overlook—and overburden. Limit yourself to a few necessities.

1. A table lamp's light can be as sleep-disruptive as a screen's glow; choose one with a dimmer switch or an adjustable neck, so you can point the beam onto the book, if you're reading.

2. Keep a water carafe and glass to quench nighttime thirst.

3. Having a personal item, such as a framed photo, flowers, or a favorite dish to hold your jewelry, will pro-mote sweet dreams.

4. Only a few books belong here—the sight of a larger stack can be a stressful reminder of those must-read titles waiting in the queue.

CLOSET

Think of your closet as a way to protect your investment—a wardrobe takes time and money to assemble. It should also be a place where you look forward to picking out what you will wear each day, even (especially!) if you have to do so in a hurry. In other words, this twice-a-day (at least) destination should marry pleasure and practicality.

MAKE IT INVITING

A closet that delights is more likely to be kept up.

- If you have a walk-in closet, build out your system over two or more walls. In a reach-in closet, create dedicated sections for rods, shelves, and drawers to make the most of a shallow space.

- White walls and other surfaces provide an airy backdrop for your clothes. Add a few accents, such as the gold hardware and ombré bins in the chic example opposite, for understated elegance.

- If space allows, include a place to perch while you try on shoes; a soft rug cushions bare feet and cozies up the space.

- Using a matching set of hangers will provide a cohesive look. Use the right type of hanger, too—wood is preferable, with clips for pants and skirts and a hanger with a bar for folding delicates over.

- Use bowls, compotes, and trays to organize fragrance bottles and loose accessories on a dresser or shelf; put jewelry you wear most often in its own dish.

- Organize hanging clothing by type—dresses to pants and skirts and then to tops—to easily find things and create a calm and cohesive look.

MAKE IT PRACTICAL

Getting dressed is so much easier when your closet is well-considered.

- In the spirit of planning ahead and easing the morning routine, create a spot for your next-day outfit—this can also go on the back of the door or on a hook in the bedroom.

- Mount a full-length mirror inside the closet or on the back of a door; hang a smaller mirror above a dresser for putting on accessories.

- Insert wooden boot shapers in tall boots to keep them from flopping over on a shelf.

- Give purses and totes their own shelves; tuck tissue into soft-sided ones to help them stand up.

- Keep a lint remover where it will get used.

- Tuck cedar or sachets filled with dried lavender and essential oils among folded knitwear to keep pests at bay.

- Keep a stepstool nearby for reaching high shelves.

WORKABLE DETAILS

Whether small or spacious, any closet can be improved with these takeaways.

1. The space-saving drop-down ledge provides a convenient place to fold clothes. A clipboard hung above it doubles as a folding board for sweaters—they'll take up less room folded properly.

2. Keeping shoes and boots off the floor gives the appearance of more space; install a shelf down below to hold them.

3. Round up all your clotheskeeping supplies and put them in the closet, such as on a dedicated shelf. Here the small box holds a sewing kit; the larger bin holds shoe polishes and cloths.

MARTHA MUST

When storing folded sweaters and other items on shelves, you can keep them from toppling over by stacking them between shelf dividers; clear acrylic dividers are nearly invisible and do not require any hardware, so you can adjust their position to accommodate different items in different seasons.

THE DETAILS: ACCESSORIES

From hats to pumps, sunglasses to strings of pearls—these are pieces that make you feel polished. Frustrating, then, that they're so easy to misplace, tangle up, or otherwise lose to disarray. Keep them straight with these smart strategies.

SCARVES AND SUNGLASSES

These are the last accessories you grab before running out the door. This space-saving, slide-out solution fits on a side wall in your closet, and keeps them within easy reach. Screw two towel rods onto a 20-by-24-inch painted wooden board, install two drawer slides to affix it to the wall, and add a drawer pull to the closer side of the board. Hang S hooks on the upper rod to hold scarves and chains, and simply hang glasses over the bar below.

JEWELRY

Skip the stacked box and create a jewelry drawer in a dresser or storage unit instead, fitting acrylic containers of various sizes inside to accommodate all your baubles, from earrings to bracelets and necklaces. Larger sections can hold sunglasses and bulkier items. This way, you'll be able to spread everything out and actually see what you have (and more quickly find what you are looking for).

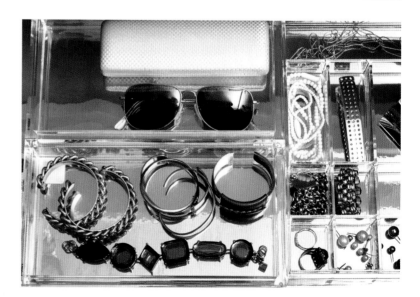

SEASONAL ITEMS

Choose color-coordinated bins to hold out-of-season items (such as summer hats in one, winter in the other) on a high shelf, adding labels for at-a-glance reminders. Lids will keep out dust and pests; wrapping each item in acid-free tissue paper will help preserve its shape and color.

SHOES

Can't live without them; can't find enough ways to store them. The key to getting and keeping shoes organized is not having every pair you own in rotation at the same time. Keep only the ones you're wearing frequently in the open—on a lower closet shelf, on a tiered freestanding unit, or in an over-the-door multipocket organizer, if space is tight. The rest belong up high, in matching clear bins or shoeboxes labeled with a photo for easy identification, or tucked into bins under the bed.

LAUNDRY ROOM

Sorting, pretreating, mending, washing, drying, folding—we do all this and more in what is often an all-too-limited area. No surprise it can be an especially chaotic part of the house. But a few simple tweaks—adding a countertop to maximize over-the-machine work space, for instance, and decanting detergent and other supplies for a unified look—will help you reimagine your own laundry room, turning it into a more enjoyable environment.

An adjacent bathroom (or hallway) can become a convenient ironing spot.

Wire bins let used towels dry before washing, to keep musty odors at bay.

Install a counter over side-by-side units for extra storage and a folding surface.

ORGANIZE YOUR HOME

ENTRYWAY

KITCHEN

BATHROOM

LIVING ROOM

BEDROOM

LAUNDRY ROOM

HOME OFFICE

KIDS' ROOMS

UTILITY SPACES

EVALUATE THE SPACE

Ample storage capacity, a surface for folding, and a place for hanging clothes are essential elements of any functional laundry room. The following are ways to boost your own room's potential, no matter how big or small.

CONSIDER YOUR REGULAR ROUTINE

Before you invest in organizing tools and supplies, ask yourself the following.

- How do you typically handle laundry chores? If it's all on one day as opposed to spreading loads out over a week, you will likely need more hampers and more space for sorting everything at once.

- Do you iron often? If so, is there room to set up an ironing board or will you need to handle that task in another, nearby space?

- It's always better to fold laundry right out of the dryer rather than have the items pile up on a bed or sofa or languish in a basket, where they'll be forgotten and end up wrinkled. You'll want a surface for this purpose; if space is too tight, a fold-down ledge will do the trick.

- Factor in how you'll hang just-dried clothes: A tension rod is easy to put up, or mount telescoping rods (used for towels in a bathroom) that swing out when needed. Freestanding clothing racks are also convenient, and can be repurposed in a guest room.

- Will other household goods, such as cleaning supplies or rolls of paper towels, be better stored here? If space allows, you could create a "surplus station" for those and any other items that otherwise don't have a home, such as in a closed cabinet, assigning different shelves to different needs.

MAKE THE MOST OF THE MACHINES

When you are ready to replace your machines, consider the following ways to get the most bang for your buck.

- Washers and dryers come in many space-saving packages—there are stackable units and compact models to choose from, as well as all-in-one machines that have ventless (plug-in) dryers. (If you do a lot of tumble-drying, however, the longer drying time of these smaller units may not be worth the trade-off in added space.)

- Front-loading washing machines have greater water-extracting functioning than top-loaders (so clothes will take less time to dry) and are the only option when it comes to washing down pillows and duvets, which tend to float and remain dry in top-loaders.

- If you have kids (and their stains), it may be worth splurging on a steam-wash unit, which blasts steam from the bottom to attack even tough spots.

TOWELS AND BED LINENS

Fold these right away—and the right way—before stashing in a linen closet or elsewhere.

- A properly folded towel has a fluffy appearance and hidden edges. First fold the towel into thirds lengthwise. (If the towel will be hung, do it now.) Then fold it into thirds the other way, creating a rectangle.

- Bind sets of guest towels (washcloth, hand towel, bath sheet) using twine or ribbon. When visitors arrive, transfer a stack from the linen closet to the guest bedroom.

- To keep bed linens organized, wrap each folded set into one of the set's pillowcases (page 25). Then coordinate sets by room or by sheet size, shelving together.

STRATEGIZE THE STORAGE

Whether it's a dedicated space or a carved-out corner in a kitchen or mudroom, the laundry room should be set up in a way that makes getting it all done less of a chore and more a labor of love.

MINE EVERY INCH

As with other living spaces, thinking vertically can often be the answer.

- Make use of a wall above the washer/dryer (or next to stacked units) by installing shelves or cabinetry for keeping supplies within easy access.

- Choose shelves that are sturdy enough to hold heavy soap containers and other supplies but not so deep that things get pushed out of reach.

- When wall space is limited, use a customizable cart with mesh drawers (often meant for kitchens or closets)—which can be topped with butcher block or another counter surface, for a folding or storage surface. Add casters for space-saving portability.

AIM FOR EFFICIENCY

Giving everything a home is a must in any organizing system, but especially for such a high-functioning room.

- Store items according to how often you use them, with occasionals (such as spare towels) on a higher shelf and your regular detergent lower down.

- It also helps to create stations by storing items by how they are used—whether for stain-fighting or mending.

- Group like items together on trays or other shallow containers, to keep them tidy and allow for easy access.

- Industrial-style steel laundry carts are convenient for rolling loads to and from the machines, and they come in different sizes to handle different loads.

- Use deep baskets or bins (ideally stackable) to cart loads of folded laundry from room to room, designating one for each location and labeling them as such (or with each person's name, so kids can pitch in).

- Store your ironing board where it's used. If you don't have room for even a folding model, try getting by with an ironing blanket—such as a thick, white cotton towel—that you can put on any flat surface, even a table. Or use a steamer instead.

- Keep a small broom and dustpan at hand to whisk away spills.

CLOSET CONVERSION

You can turn any space—one end of a mudroom or even a spare closet—into a highly functional laundry room.

1. Wide shelving provides generous storage, and Shaker-style pegs offer spots for cleaning tools, hangers, and a handy stain-removal chart.

2. Group like items together (lint brushes, stain-fighting solutions) in separate containers, to keep them tidy and allow for easy access.

3. Create a work space atop the washer/dryer units. Here the placement of the muslin-covered board makes for convenient ironing.

4. Squeeze in a storage cabinet, if you can—it's nice to have an extra surface for sorting and folding. Stock wicker baskets with washable fabric liners to hold folded items.

HOME OFFICE

Whether it's command central for managing
the household or your headquarters as you punch
the proverbial nine-to-five clock, this room is
where serious business gets done. It might be a
dedicated room or a corner in a shared space, but
either way, function comes first. Just don't go so
utilitarian with it that you don't want to spend time
there. Follow these tips for creating a purposeful
yet pleasing, streamlined yet engaging space.

Use strategic pops of color—here, from the three vinyl bulletin boards—to perk up a white space and create a graphic (i.e., cool and collected) result.

The ideal desk lamp position? The light should be higher than your head but not directly in your eyeline.

Use a tiered inbox and wall-mounted file sorter to keep papers in check.

01
SEPTEMBER

EVAl

If your h
you'll wa
room sh

DEFINE

How you
the best

■ **The ful**
work rem
of your h
storage—
top of the
physical

■ **The ho**
If this is p
bills, mar
appointm
to-day ta
desk in a
want som
blends in
spill over

■ **The mu**
When knit
other hobl
office, it is
zone for th
workstatic
room. Cral
lot of stora
brand of o

■ **The fan**
place whe
work, you'
and organ
capacities
things at tl
and labelir
stand and

DESK

Disarray hinders productivity. Do the following to create a work environment that's conducive to getting things done.

BE A MINIMALIST

Keep only what you need and use regularly on top of the desk. To determine what that truly is, follow the below steps.

■ Start with only the essentials: a task lamp, computer, and writing implements and papers.

■ Move everything else on your desk into a box. Keep it within easy reach for a week (longer if you don't use the office every day).

■ Take note of how often you reach for something from the box—and gradually return only the must-haves to your desk. Anything you haven't touched can be stored.

■ To maintain a clean work space, consider using the above-desk wall space for keeping things in sight and within reach.

■ Repeat this process when you feel your desk is getting too crowded.

CONTAIN THE ODDS AND ENDS

Give everything a place on the desktop, with nothing floating about.

■ Corral like items (pens and pencils, scissors and straightedges, binder clips and paper clips) in their own vessels.

■ Don't compromise your sense of style: Use containers that are as attractive as they are functional.

■ Look around your own home and upcycle items from the kitchen or potting shed (think jars and garden tins).

■ If you are right-handed, keep all the supplies on the right side, and vice versa. Exception: The task lamp should be on the opposite side, to avoid shadows.

CURATE THE PAPERWORK

Piles visually aid your memory, but only when they are intentional—and tidy.

■ The number of piles you need or want can vary, but two reliable ones are "to do" and "in progress."

■ Save desk space with stackable solutions such as filing boxes or slotted letter bins.

■ Go paperless as much as possible; scan or snap a photo and file papers digitally (page 159).

PERSONALIZE THE SPACE

The occasional personal touch can make you feel more at ease, inspiring greater focus.

■ Houseplants, photos, collectibles, travel keepsakes, or favorite books and periodicals can make the space more inviting.

■ An inspiration board offers a visual boost to keep you motivated, and provides a way to declutter a desk and house beloved items (photos, postcards, pretty papers, and other ephemera).

■ Rotate the objects once a season—or after a big project—to keep the space feeling fresh.

PROJECT

BUNGEE-CORD SHELVES

Use molding and bungee cords to create a flexible display.

1. Buy inexpensive basics from the hardware store—strips of L-shaped corner molding, hooked bungee cords, and mounting hardware—or sub in easy-to-install picture-rail ledges.

2. Paint molding or ledges, bungee-cord hooks, and cup hooks as desired using craft or latex paint and foam applicators (here the cup hooks were painted to match the cord hardware).

3. Install cup hooks so the cords stretch tight with just a little slack; here that's 4 to 5 inches beyond edge of molding on either side.

4. Display favorite notebooks, periodicals, and such that would otherwise be buried in a stack or drawer.

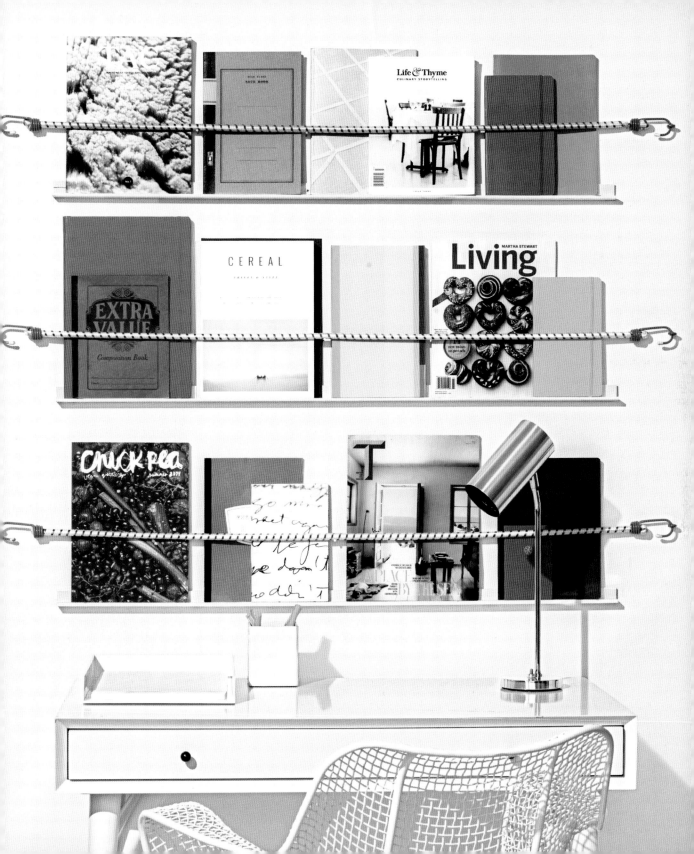

THE DETAILS: DESK ACCESSORIES

Giving everything a home—an organizing mantra worth embracing—is so much easier
to do when you employ handsome (and right-size!) containers. The sort-and-store principle will
help you get and keep your supplies in order.

DESKTOP HOLDERS

When drawer space is lacking, it's even
more important to tame the essentials
on your desktop. Here are examples of
the right tools for every job: Little lidded
containers keep thumbtacks sorted and
spill-free; a wooden tray with a tapered
edge stops washi tape from rolling away;
and a cluster of copper-plated cylinders
sort out the rest. You can find similarly
stylish options in a range of other materials to suit your space, in stainless steel,
wood, ceramic, lacquer, or acrylic.

DIY POCKET

Basic canvas paintbrush rolls, like the one
shown here, are available at art supply and
crafts stores—or sew your own from a
favorite fabric. Then add a grommet to
either side, at the top, and hang the roll on
the wall above or near your workstation,
using cup hooks (they just screw into the
wall). Easy-to-use grommet kits are available
online and at home-improvement stores.
Slide in pens and pencils, scissors, and other
slender items. Still need more storage? Hang
up two side by side or in a column.

TRAY DEPOT

Almost any room could benefit from having a tray or two to rein in its various effects—including the home office. (And should you lack a designated office, a tray can actually double as a portable desk.) A tray with high sides will contain laptops or iPads along with receipts and other ephemera, here stashed in sleek pouches and pencil cases. Handles are convenient for carting the tray around the house, and the tray can be used anywhere from ottoman to bed. What's more, it can be tucked away on a shelf or inside a credenza when the work-day is done.

DRAWER STORAGE

Fishing through a pile of office supplies for a paper clip or sticky note is time wasted, especially when it's easy to keep your drawers straightened: Sort all the odds and ends into standard-issue drawer inserts or dividers—or with individual vessels that are pretty enough to leave on the desktop while you're working. These brass-and-linen containers nestle together to keep from sliding around. You could also put an underused collection of small bowls to work to achieve the same organizational bliss.

TECHNOLOGY

Optimize the performance of your electronics with some dedicated hardware maintenance. Take care when cleaning all the components—particularly any internal parts—to avoid damaging anything. Never use harsh cleaning sprays or abrasive cleansers, and remember to unplug before you begin.

PHONE AND TABLET

Power down the device before cleaning; keep it in a case to protect against routine wear and tear.

Daily: Wipe the screen with a soft cloth, such as an eyeglass shammy. **Weekly:** Remove device from case. Lightly spray a lint-free cloth (never the phone) with a solution of equal parts distilled water and 70 percent isopropyl alcohol, then wipe down the entire device. **As needed:** Soak the case in warm, soapy water and dry thoroughly before replacing.

COMPUTER, KEYBOARD, AND MOUSE

These get touched—a lot. Rubbing alcohol evaporates quickly, so you don't have to worry about it ruining the parts. **Daily:** Spray the keyboard and mouse with a can of compressed air (fitted with an extension tube); then flip the keyboard over and gently shake to dislodge any remaining dirt. **Weekly:** Wipe the keyboard and mouse with a cloth that's been moistened with rubbing alcohol, or use a sanitizing wipe. Remove stubborn stains between keys with a cotton swab dipped in alcohol and squeezed so it's just damp.

MONITOR

Clean the screen only when it's cool and only with light pressure. Don't use ammonia- or alcohol-based products, which can damage monitors; paper towels are also too abrasive.

Daily: Dust off the screen with a microfiber cloth. **Weekly:** Use an antimicrobial spray that's specifically designed for technology (sold at office-supply stores), wiping dry with a soft cloth.

PRINTER

Models differ (and some are even self-cleaning), so check the owner's manual for specific cleaning and maintenance instructions. Never clean the interior, aside from the cartridge.

Daily: Keep the printer covered when not in use to prevent dust and dirt buildup. **Weekly:** Moisten a soft cloth with water and wipe down the exterior of the machine, as well as the paper rollers; use a moistened cotton swab for hard-to-reach areas. Spray the fan and vent with compressed air.

SHREDDER

Refer to the manual for specific instructions (and check that the unit is not plugged in).

Daily: Carefully clear any paper from the blade; consider keeping it covered to protect against dust and dirt. **Weekly:** Wipe exterior with a moistened soft cloth. **As needed:** Run a lubricating sheet, sold at office-supply stores, through the shredder to keep blades sharp.

DIGITAL DESKTOP

Your virtual desktop can accumulate a lot of clutter and slow your system down. Spend 10 to 15 minutes each week cleaning it up with the following tips in mind.

- Start by purging: Move files you no longer need from your desktop and downloads folder to the trash. Uninstall any apps or software programs you never use.

- Simplify your desktop: Treat this as a temporary parking space; only save files here that need attention right away.

- Protect your files: Make sure to regularly back them up (especially personal documents and photos); there are many convenient cloud-based storage options to choose from.

KIDS' ROOMS

These rooms present their own organizing challenges. Namely: how to deal with a mountain of toys, a surplus of crafts supplies, a steady stream of artwork, and all the homework essentials, plus an ever-changing wardrobe. The room itself needs to evolve over the years, too—something to keep in mind when picking color schemes and furniture pieces. Here are tips for creating inspiring bedrooms and play spaces that are also practical—and tricks for keeping them that way.

Having a theme—here, a love for animals—gives the space more meaning.

You can replicate this built-in with freestanding bookshelves and wall-mounted shelves.

Neutral shades are less likely to become outgrown or outdated; pillows and other objects inject color and personality.

Unify a collection of mismatched chairs and a table, found at flea markets, with a coat of paint in the same shade.

EVALUATE THE SPACE

A kid's bedroom needs to provide maximum storage capacity with minimal upkeep. It also needs to be adaptable over time—and to make way for lots of fun! You can accomplish all these things by doing your homework before you start.

MATCH FORM WITH FUNCTION

Just because it's a kid's room doesn't mean it has to be childish. They grow up so fast! Organize with long-lasting style and different functions in mind.

- Unless you have a dedicated playroom, a kid's bedroom will need to serve multiple purposes. Creating stations—arts and crafts, reading (for fun), schoolwork, hobbies—will encourage kids to engage in different activities and help them stay focused when they do.

- Reading is something kids never outgrow. Even if you don't have a built-in space (such as the one opposite), you can create an inviting reading nook by putting floor pillows in a corner with adequate lighting and some (but not an overabundance of) books within easy reach, rotating those out to keep the selection fresh.

- A crafts area promotes open-ended creativity; all it takes is a table and some basic supplies (see page 256 for a list of those and page 168 for storage ideas).

- As for any other room, including objects that are aesthetically appealing and create a sense of order (such as the ceramics, matching set of raffia bins, and color-coded book jackets shown here) will enhance kids' overall enjoyment and boost their productivity (and mood), even if they don't consciously realize it.

GIVE THEM ROOM TO GROW

Just when you find the perfect bed/desk/dresser, your kid has outgrown it (or the design). Buy pieces that will grow with your kids to avoid that dilemma.

- Start with the nursery: There are convertible cribs that switch to toddler beds, and changing tables that double as dressers (remove the protective top).

- Some toddler beds fold down to be full length but narrower than a twin, leaving you with more floor space for at least several more years (and during the time when kids use floors the most).

- Look for "activity" tables that come with two leg lengths—one accommodates play chairs; the other standard seating, and built-in storage.

- Bunk beds and loft beds are great space-saving options so long as you observe safety precautions, including having guardrails securely in place (check frequently) and the top part mounted to the wall (using the proper hardware). The American Academy of Pediatrics suggests children be at least 6 years old before sleeping on the top bunk or in a loft bed; you should also consider your child's sleep patterns, keeping anyone who is prone to sleepwalking or multiple bathroom visits on the bottom bunk until older. Always get a parent's permission before allowing a friend to sleep on the upper bunk.

CLOSET TIPS

For such little people, kids can accumulate a lot of clothes.

- Buy only what's needed to get through each season at a time. That could mean five (each) tops and bottoms for school, plus one or two "dress-up" outfits and a couple of sweaters or jackets for cool-weather layering.

- Hang clothes when possible—this frees up drawers and cubbies for other items. If there's no closet, you could mount some cute hooks along a wall.

- Athletic apparel and casual tops and bottoms can be rolled up to save space.

- Consider fitting one side of the closet with shelves and drawers, avoiding the need for dressers and making it easier for kids to find and put away their clothes.

BOOKS AND TOYS

The goal: For kids to read and play whenever the mood strikes, and without having to ask for help in finding what they want or putting things back. The plan: Work as a team to design a system that suits you both, employing the tips below.

SORT AND STORE

- Together, go through all the various items—toys, books, stuffed animals—and group into categories (cars in one pile, Legos in another). Have your child show you where different groups best belong.

- Use bins and/or baskets (clear ones let them see what's inside) to house different items, then allow kids to design the labels with words or drawings.

- Keeping books and puzzles and interactive toys within easy reach will encourage frequent use. Stash less desirable (according to you!) toys on a higher shelf.

ENLIST HELP WITH UPKEEP

- Teach your kids that "once you play, you then sort and put away." (Rhyming is not only fun, it helps kids remember the rules.) Be sure to offer plenty of positive reinforcement for keeping on track—whether that's a star chart or getting to choose the movie for family film night.

- For books, you may want to relax the "put away" rule a bit, since putting titles away may mean never pulling them out again. In this case, try creating zones, such as "currently reading" on a nightstand, "next up" on a play table or lower bookshelf (apart from the others), and "all-time favorites" that may merit being on permanent display—on a special floating shelf, for example.

- Conduct monthly check-ins to make sure things are being put away correctly and to see if anything needs adjusting—kids' interests can change quickly, meaning last month's Lincoln Logs are now taking up valuable space for this month's erector sets.

PLAN AHEAD

- Enforce the "one in, one out" rule. Before your kid gets to bring home a new toy or gadget she simply cannot live without, strike a bargain by having her choose one existing item to give away—and it has to be of equal value (so no pencil eraser from a party-favor bag in exchange for a dancing robot).

- Kids tend to accumulate lots of tchotchkes. At the beginning of each year (or during the holidays), give each child a memory box to put favorite keepsakes in; at the end of the year, label it and put it on a high shelf—out of the way but still within sight in case he wants to revisit those items now and then.

CUBBY STATION

Making this freestyle storage unit is half the fun—arrange the wooden boxes, sold at crafts stores and online, however you like. Be sure to mount them securely to the wall using screws and anchors designed for the wall's surface (and caution kids not to climb on them).

1. Use hooks, tacks, or elastic cord to create even more storage opportunities on the exteriors of the boxes (for displaying favorite creations); outfit the interiors with customized organizers.

2. Paint the boxes in different hues to expedite cleanup (so the yellow containers go in the yellow box).

3. Include a wood-framed chalkboard and a pinup board to showcase still more creations.

ARTS AND CRAFTS

If kids know where to find everything—the colored pencils are always here, the modeling clay there—they will be more inclined to use it all in exercising their creative muscles. Seeing their own handiwork on display will also motivate them to continue these worthwhile pursuits.

KEEP SUPPLIES UNDER CONTROL

Be sure to do this exercise together to avoid the all-too-common "where's my [fill in the blank]?!" See pages 170 to 171 for more ideas and inspiration.

■ Group like with like, so all paints in one bin, papers in another; magazine holders can keep different kinds of paper stock in check.

■ Decant crayons, colored pencils, and markers into separate vessels (one for each category), for easier grabbing.

■ Store the essentials for favorite activities in project-based bins—one for jewelry-making, for example.

■ Clear containers—plastic bins, large (recycled) jars, food-storage containers, or a combination—keep supplies visible at all times.

■ Look for crafts tables that come with storage space, such as a ledge underneath—or repurpose a bilevel coffee table, which is just the right height for toddlers.

■ If space is especially tight, use an over-the-door shoe organizer to hold supplies of all sorts; mount a file sorter on a wall or door to streamline papers.

CURATE THE ARTWORK

Most young kids are pretty prolific—and you'll want to motivate them to continue these worthwhile pursuits.

■ Plan to go through the collection with your child at least twice a year (say, at the end of each school semester), letting them choose the ones they want to keep and also to put on display.

■ Besides posting on the refrigerator, consider framing a few select pieces and working those into a gallery wall—or dedicate an entire wall to their creations (as shown opposite).

■ Preserve favorite pieces in flat archival boxes or acid-free portfolios, both of which come in a range of sizes; note your child's name and age on a small label, or write directly on the back of the piece. Or scan items when possible and save them digitally, organizing these as above—by child and by year.

■ Then look for ways to upcycle the originals—as well as any pieces that don't make the cut: Use them for paper-craft projects, cards, or wrapping paper.

PROJECT

GRAPHIC GRID

Here's a display that lets you swap out pieces whenever the artistic mood strikes.

1. Using a level, yard-stick or ruler, and pencil, first plot out a grid on the wall in the desired pattern.

2. Adhere painted lattice strips (from a home-improvement store) to wall with glue and nails. Or use ribbon and thumbtacks as an alternative.

3. Screw bulldog clips to the lattice (or nail to the wall if using ribbon) to hold a rotating selection of art and other items, such as the supply holders above the crafts table.

THE DETAILS: CRAFT SUPPLIES

Here are four ways to encourage kids to unleash their creativity by putting tools at their fingertips. Giving each item its own storage spot will make it easy for toddlers to teens to put things back where they belong.

DIY DRAWER

Why not encourage creativity while fostering independence at the same time? Stash crafts essentials along with kid-friendly practical items in the kitchen, and you'll have the answer to "I'm bored!" and "I'm hungry!" all in one spot. Designate a drawer within the reach of your littlest family members, and outfit it with colorful dividers to separate the unbreakable cups, bowls, and water bottles they'll need at snack time from supplies like paper, markers, pencils, paints, and safety scissors that will keep their hands busy as you handle food prep.

LOCKER BINS

You can find old-fashioned lockers in all dimensions and orientations, including this horizontal version—which can double as a bench, with or without a cushion on top. It has convenient slots for stashing assorted papers and note-books, plus room for bins, with labels to identify the supplies inside. Magnetic locker organizers (the same kind used for school lockers) help keep smaller supplies within easy reach inside the doors. Decorative stickers are optional!

SHELF HELP

For older kids, create a craft station in a bedroom, family room, or office with a shelf and some glass jars. Use the under-shelf space to double the storage: Start by screwing the lids into the shelf (drill a pilot hole and secure them with anchors for more stability), placing two screws evenly within the diameter; or you can try using strong adhesive tabs for a more temporary (and easier-to-do) solution. Then fill the jars and twist them in place. More jars and other holders can rest up top; suction hooks can keep scissors and hole punches in place. Round out the makeshift craft area with inspirational images on the surrounding wall.

COLORING WALL

Your kids will love having a larger canvas to work with. Start with one of your child's own creations or draw one yourself (black-and-white pictures work best). Then supersize it:

1. Bring the drawing to a print shop to have the image enlarged, using a large-format copier, to a three-by-four-foot print or even larger (it's inexpensive to do).

2. Tape it to the wall of their bedroom or playroom using low-tack painter's tape, provide washable markers or crayons, and let the coloring begin.

EVALUATE THE SPACE

The goal: Store items so you can quickly find them when you need them—whether you're packing for summer camp or decorating the house for the holidays.

PURGE

In these storage spaces, excess stuff piles up fast.

- At least once a year, take inventory of the attic, garage, and basement and earmark items to donate or sell. This includes clothing and toys, luggage, furniture, household goods, bicycles and sporting gear, and tools and machinery in good condition that your family has either outgrown or replaced. Schedule this exercise before organizing a tag sale.

- Anything that is beyond repair should be discarded. If you have old paint or other hazardous substances, check with your local municipality about special rules for disposal.

- If you have years of boxes to go through, consider renting a small dumpster, which can be dropped off and picked up by the company; visit thebagster.com for an even more affordable alternative.

- Keep extra "donate," "sell," and "toss" bins in each space at all times, so you can weed out items whenever you go to dig something out. This will make the once-yearly purging less painful.

SORT

Once you've whittled the "to keep" contents down, group them into categories.

- Draw up a blueprint of each space, creating zones for each category, so you know where everything goes.

- Stackable clear plastic bins with tight-fitting lids offer better protection against the elements and pests and are sturdier than cardboard boxes; plus, you can see what's inside.

- Label everything! Even if you think you'll remember what's in each box or bin. Label individual paint cans, too, so you can remember where each is used.

- Plan to keep items you often need, such as extra place settings or gift wrapping supplies, in an accessible location, like in a cabinet near the entrance.

STORE

Keep as much off the floor as possible. Flooding, pests, and dust and dirt are all risk factors.

- Metal shelving is affordable, adjustable, and easy to assemble—plus, it can withstand heat and humidity. Open shelving is also helpful for finding things.

- That said, if you have little ones around, you should lock up any hazardous items in a cabinet. Likewise for storing extra household paper goods and pet food or other items that attract pests.

- Install racks on the ceiling of the garage for hanging out-of-season recreational gear or extension work ladders that you don't use every day.

- Because of the temperature and humidity fluctuations of attics and basements, avoid storing valuable or sentimental pieces there.

HARD-WORKING WORKSHOP

If you are handy around the house, it's worth setting up a dedicated station.

- Group the essentials in one corner of the garage or shed, dividing it into zones—painting and hardware, for example.

- Equip the space with electrical outlets for power tools and adequate lighting.

- Keep supplies at eye level with shelves on a wall-mounted track system.

- Add a framed sheet of pegboard over the bench to hold tools.

- Use assorted hooks to hold a ladder, safety gear, and sawhorses.

- Consider mounting a magnetic knife rack to safely hold sharp tools like saws.

STRATEGIZE THE STORAGE

Here are time-tested methods for storing the most common categories of items so they are preserved and protected for the long term. If you live in a damp environment, it's worth investing in a dehumidifier for these spaces, especially a basement.

CLOTHING AND LINENS

Avoid storing these items where they will be subjected to excessive humidity, such as in an unfinished basement.

- Properly launder all your woolens before storing— hats and gloves, scarves and sweaters.

- Take coats outside and brush vigorously under the collar and around the seams (where moth eggs or larvae like to live).

- Thoroughly clean winter footwear with a stiff brush; stuff boots with tissue paper to retain their shape.

- Hang coats in canvas storage bags. Add cedar blocks or lavender sachets to keep pests at bay (avoid mothballs and moth crystals, which contain pesticides that can be harmful to people and pets).

- Store folded items (sweaters, scarves, bedding) in tightly sealed plastic containers.

TOYS

Keep outdoor toys and out-of-season playthings in one handy spot.

- An open shelving unit, such as the steel model above, has adjustable shelves that can be changed over time— you can switch out toys for items like luggage, coolers, or bulk cleaning supples.

- To replicate the look, pick up a bunch of wooden crates (look for them at tag sales and flea markets) and paint them in the desired shades. Or purchase color-coordinated bins.

- Sort the toys by category and label bins accordingly, keeping favorite toys on lower shelves where kids can easily reach them. Have a stool on hand for getting at those items on a higher shelf. Be sure to use safety brackets to secure shelves to walls.

SPORTS GEAR

A garage or mudroom offers grab-and-go convenience.

- Good old-fashioned lockers have hooks for hanging uniforms and adjustable shelves for shoes and more. Mount magnetic hooks outside for holding lacrosse sticks (or other gear that doesn't fit inside) and a mesh bag for containing balls.

- The shelving unit shown here can also organize items by sport and hold lawn games for the whole family.

PART THREE

ORGANIZE YOUR ROUTINE

With some proactive planning, it's entirely possible to skillfully manage the details of your life—from cleaning the home to helping children with homework to tending the garden to having friends over for dinner. Streamlining each task to do it as efficiently as possible—and organizing everything on checklists according to daily, weekly, or yearly schedules— ensures that nothing gets overlooked and you don't feel overburdened, even when hosting Thanksgiving or checking off your holiday gift list.

CLEAN

When cleaning the house, adhere to
some time-tested methods: If your
supplies are hardworking multitaskers,
you won't need as many of them;
if your techniques are efficient, your
efforts will pay off more quickly.
And, of course, a schedule is key—follow
the streamlined-but-thorough routine
outlined here, and you'll have
more time to simply enjoy your home.

3. GO FROM TOP TO BOTTOM

Dust and dirt are subject to gravity just like everything else.

- Start on the top floor of the home and work your way down—this way you won't be tracking dirt.

- Hit the hallways and staircases along the way, cleaning the baseboards, risers, and handrails (not just the stair treads).

- Clean from ceiling to floor in individual rooms: Dust the ceiling lights and fans, then the window frames, furniture, and radiators—and, finally, the floors.

- All rules have exceptions: When washing off walls, starting at the top will only result in dirty lower reaches—clean these from bottom to top.

4. WORK FROM THE INSIDE OUT

This method is a must for sweeping, mopping, or vacuuming, but it helps establish a rhythm for general tidying up, too.

TIP

When mopping wood floors, go with the grain; for other surfaces, work the string mop in overlapping figure eight motions to avoid streaking. Start by sweeping or vacuuming, especially in the corners, to keep dust and dirt from scratching the surfaces.

- Emptying the trash, going for more cleaning supplies, answering the doorbell—these and other distractions often cause you to leave a room during cleaning, thereby disturbing an already cleaned entrance.

- Instead, start by cleaning rooms from the point farthest from the door, toting your cleaning caddy with you.

- In pass-through spaces, do the reverse: Start by cleaning at the entry point and then work your way to the exit point, where you will then clean that adjacent room.

5. CLEAN DRY, THEN WET

There's no other way to keep everyday grime, pet hair, and food crumbs from spreading around.

- This principle applies particularly to bathrooms: Dust all surfaces thoroughly (it's easy to forget this step in this space) and then sweep (or vacuum) the floor before washing down the sink, tub, and toilet. End with wet-mopping.

- Repeat the above in the kitchen, sweeping off counters and tables and floors before using wet methods on sinks, stoves, and appliances.

- Always thoroughly sweep, run a microfiber mop, or vacuum before wet-mopping the floor in any space. You'll also save time and effort (filling the bucket and such) by waiting to wet-mop all floors in the home at the end, going back through from top to bottom and following your usual order.

DIY CLEANSERS

Save money (and the planet) with these solutions, adding essential oil for all-natural scent.

- All-purpose cleaner: Mix 2 tablespoons mild dishwashing liquid or pure castile soap with 2 cups water in a spray bottle.

- Glass cleaner: Mix equal parts white vinegar and hot water in a spray bottle; wipe with a microfiber cloth or reuseable paper towel.

- Scouring cleaner: Mix three parts warm water with one part baking soda; add a few drops of dishwashing liquid or castile soap for a tougher (but scratch-free) sink-and-tub paste. Or dip the cut side of a lemon half in coarse salt and scrub with that—great for scouring cutting boards and removing tarnish from copper.

SCHEDULE

Use the following schedule to help you maintain your cleaning routine. Here are helpful tips to check off your daily, weekly, even once- or twice-yearly lists.

DAILY

- ☐ Make bed.
- ☐ Clean as you cook.
- ☐ Unload dishwasher.
- ☐ Rinse and wring out sponges.
- ☐ Wipe down all sinks plus kitchen counters and backsplash.
- ☐ Sweep floors—especially in the kitchen.
- ☐ After each use, squeegee shower walls, close liner, and run exhaust fan or open windows for 30 minutes.
- ☐ Put away clothes.
- ☐ Clean out dryer vent after each load.

WEEKLY

- ☐ Dust tables and other surfaces, including picture frames and shelves.
- ☐ Wipe down small kitchen appliances, such as the toaster or coffee maker.
- ☐ Clean electronics, using compressed air and a soft cloth.

- ☐ Vacuum floors and area rugs.
- ☐ Mop sealed floors.
- ☐ Vacuum upholstery, using the crevice tool to reach tight spaces.
- ☐ Scrub bathroom surfaces; clean mirrors throughout the house.

EVERY OTHER WEEK

- ☐ Replace or sanitize sponges.
- ☐ Dust lighting fixtures and lightbulbs.
- ☐ Clean around baseboards with unscented dryer sheets or damp cloths.

MONTHLY

- ☐ Replace baking soda box in refrigerator to deodorize.
- ☐ Vacuum blinds and curtains with the soft-brush attachment.

- ☐ Dust ceiling fans (page 46).
- ☐ Vacuum ceilings and walls.
- ☐ Dust houseplants; wipe down leaves with a damp cloth.
- ☐ Clean tile grout: Apply a baking soda paste; spray with vinegar. Let sit (and fizz); scrub with a soft toothbrush, then rinse with a damp rag.
- ☐ Deodorize and disinfect sink and tub drains: Pour in a pot of boiling water, add 1 cup baking soda, then 1 cup vinegar; cover, let sit 10 minutes, then flush with more boiling water.
- ☐ Soak kids' bath toys in a solution of ½ cup vinegar per gallon of warm water for up to an hour; scrub with a sponge.

MARTHA MUST

Storing all your cleaning supplies in a bucket, such as the one you use for mopping, makes it easy to tote them where they're needed. Also, be sure to keep it in a central location, for all-points access.

If you have 5 minutes…

- Clean bathroom mirrors and wipe down sink.
- Wipe down kitchen sink and counters.
- Pick up items from floor and put where they belong.

If you have 10 minutes…

- Dust surfaces in your common areas.
- Clean out drawers in refrigerator.

If you have 15 minutes…

- Sweep and mop (or just vacuum) floors.

- ☐ Sweep and dust basement and attic.

ONCE A SEASON

- ☐ Edit pantry, discarding any expired items (page 112).
- ☐ Freshen dishwasher: Sprinkle 1 cup baking soda on the bottom (or put 1 cup white vinegar on the lower rack). Run empty machine on a short hot-water cycle.

- [ ] Deodorize garbage disposal: Grind vinegar ice cubes or citrus peels in it.
- [ ] Clean interior of garbage bin with warm soapy water.
- [ ] Deep-clean range hood and inside of oven (page 79).
- [ ] Descale showerheads (plus tub and sink faucets): Submerge attached head in a plastic bag filled with vinegar; secure with rubber bands. Leave 30 minutes or overnight. Remove bag; scrub with a soft toothbrush, then rinse.
- [ ] Dust bookshelves: Vacuum tops and spines of books. Remove books and wipe the shelf with a damp cloth.
- [ ] Vacuum and rotate mattresses.
- [ ] Deep-clean washing machine: Add 2 cups vinegar to detergent dispenser during a hot-water cycle, then do another hot-water cycle with ¼ cup baking soda added to drum.
- [ ] Clean dehumidifier: Wash water tank and filter with warm soapy water.

PATIOS AND PORCHES

Give your outdoor spaces a little TLC.

ROUTINE CARE
1. Sweep floors with an outdoor push broom.
2. Dust windowsills, doorframes, and ceiling fan blades using a counter (aka bench) brush.

SEASONAL MAINTENANCE
1. Sweep away cobwebs and debris with a corn broom.
2. Wash down walls with diluted all-purpose cleaner and a large polyester sponge.
3. Scrub flooring with a long-handled deck brush and all-purpose cleaner mixed with hot water.
4. Scrub away any mildew from surfaces with 1 cup oxygen bleach per gallon of water (wear gloves and goggles).
5. Clean porch screens with all-purpose cleaner (avoid one with ammonia if you have aluminum screens) and a scrub brush. Rinse thoroughly with a garden hose; allow to air-dry.
6. Repaint floors (and steps) as needed. First sand existing paint, sweep away debris, and clean with diluted all-purpose cleaner; then rinse, and wait until dry before applying paint.

TWICE A YEAR
- [ ] Wash exterior siding (page 42).
- [ ] Wash windows; clean screens or storm windows before storing.
- [ ] Deep-clean refrigerator and freezer.
- [ ] Vacuum around dryer and vents.
- [ ] Clean basement: Vacuum floors, ceilings, and walls; clean windows.
- [ ] Discard expired cosmetics (page 120) and medications.
- [ ] Clean vents: Remove and soak covers in warm soapy water, scrubbing with a soft-bristled brush; let air-dry. Vacuum unit with crevice tool, then replace cover.
- [ ] Deep-clean bookshelves (page 24).

ONCE A YEAR
- [ ] Steam-clean carpet, rugs, curtains, and upholstery (first check fabric-care label, as some textiles should be serviced by a professional).
- [ ] Have HVAC ducts cleaned.

3. WASH

- When doing back-to-back loads, start with cold-water cycles and end with the hottest.

- Today's high-efficiency machines have a great deal of agitating power and require much less detergent to get clothes clean; if you have one, be sure to choose a low-sudsing product labeled for "He" use.

- Borax also helps detergent work harder, dispersing it more evenly and also tackling stains.

- Add ¼ cup white vinegar to the rinse cycle for softer towels and bedding.

- Don't overfill the machine. Fewer loads may sound tempting, but it's at the risk of wearing out the items (due to more friction) and not having them get truly clean.

- Use the shortest wash cycle (except for very soiled items) and rinse with cold water—it will save you time and money and still get the job done.

- Hand-wash delicate items—lingerie, tights, fine knitwear—or launder them in zippered mesh bags on the "delicates" or "hand-wash" cycle.

4. DRY

- Air-dry when possible, either on a clothesline (check local regulations) or an indoor wooden rack, giving each item a good shake to smooth out wrinkles. You can also hang blouses and dresses on hangers to dry.

- To soften items that are stiff after air-drying (towels and denim), tumble-dry briefly while still damp.

- When tumble-drying clothes and bedding, use the gentlest cycle and lowest heat possible.

- To extend the life of bedding and minimize wrinkles, take items out of the dryer right away—and avoid overdrying (use the moisture sensor); put sheets on beds and cases on pillows while still warm.

- Make a habit of cleaning out the dryer's lint filter after each use. If your dryer seems slow, that's likely the cause.

---

5. FOLD/HANG

- Fold or hang clothes fresh from the dryer to avoid wrinkling—and clear the drying rack once clothes are dry (and before doing another load).

- It helps to have a surface for folding right in the laundry area, either on top of the machines or a drop-down ledge.

- Put folded items in drawers or closets right away—don't let them pile up.

- You may want to sort items into baskets and let kids fold and put away their own clothes—making sure they can reach drawers and shelves (provide a stool) and hanging rods; use labels so they know where everything goes.

- Always hang skirts and pants on hangers with clips to maintain their drape and any pleats—put a cotton pad between the clip and fabric to prevent dents.

6. PRESS

- Smaller washloads can mean fewer wrinkles—as does removing items right after washing and drying (or while still damp in the case of sheets and pillowcases).

- A steamer is gentle enough to work on even delicate fabrics but powerful enough to smooth out wrinkles from all but the most durable cottons and wrinkle-prone linens. Plus, there's no board to contend with—you can steam clothes right on their hangers, and sheets on a bed.

- That said, if you want crisp creases in your shirts or tablecloths, an iron is still the best tool. Organize your items from delicates or less wrinkled to sturdy or most wrinkled so the iron will be hot enough by the time it needs to be.

- For nearly wrinkle-free clothes in a pinch, pop them into the dryer with a clean, damp towel for a few minutes.

SCHEDULE

In a busy, multiperson household, dirty clothes can pile up fast. Doing the rest of the laundry (bed linens, towels) on a regular timeline will help you keep it all in check.

DAILY

- ☐ Put dirty laundry in hampers.
- ☐ Make the bed.
- ☐ Leave the door and detergent cover of washing machine open after each cycle (to prevent mold and mildew).
- ☐ Empty dryer's lint filter.
- ☐ Hang up towels to dry after using.
- ☐ Spray shower-curtain liner with equal parts white vinegar and water after each use.

If you have 5 minutes…
- • Check rooms for dirty laundry.
- • Replenish supplies.

If you have 10 minutes…
- • Inspect items in hamper for tears.
- • Pretreat any stains.

If you have 15 minutes…
- • Hand-wash delicates.
- • Strip beds and put on fresh linens.

WEEKLY

- ☐ Wash towels in warm water.
- ☐ Launder sheets and pillowcases (and comforter cover every other week if you forgo a top sheet) in warm water.
- ☐ Wash, dry, fold/hang, press, and put away clothing.

TWICE MONTHLY

- ☐ Wash bath mats in warm water.

MONTHLY

- ☐ Launder pillow and mattress protectors in warm water.
- ☐ Fluff pillows and comforters in the dryer (using low heat and adding a damp cloth).
- ☐ Wash shower-curtain liner in hot water (with a couple of old towels for more abrasion). Add ½ cup white vinegar to rinse cycle. Hang it up to air-dry.
- ☐ Launder fabric shower curtain in warm water on a gentle cycle; hang it up to air-dry

or tumble-dry on low heat.

ONCE A SEASON

- ☐ Wash pillows and comforters (page 189).
- ☐ Vacuum dryer's lint drawer.
- ☐ Descale iron if the plate feels sticky or leaves marks on items; check owner's manual for cleaning instructions.

TWICE A YEAR

- ☐ Air out pillows and comforters on a dry, sunny day.

- ☐ Launder furniture slipcovers (or take to a professional dry cleaner). Remove from dryer while still damp, replace on the chair or sofa, and let dry overnight.
- ☐ Hand-wash woolens before storing for the off-season.

ONCE A YEAR

- ☐ Replace cover for ironing board (if you iron often); otherwise, do this as needed.

GARDEN

No matter how green your thumb,
a gardener is constantly learning—there
is always some new method to
master or rare specimen to discover.
At any level, success takes
the right tools and techniques, and
a fair amount of practice using them.
Whether you're cultivating a
landscape, nurturing a cutting
garden, or even just tending a budding
collection of houseplants, the
strategies here will keep you growing.

SUPPLIES

You can tackle most gardening tasks (digging, planting, pruning) with the essentials; pick up any extras as you go, to ease your efforts.

ESSENTIALS	EXTRAS
☐ Gardening gloves	☐ Garden fork (for turning soil)
☐ Hand cultivator	☐ Hedge shears
☐ Handsaw (for pruning branches)	☐ Hori hori (weeding knife)
☐ Hoe (for weeding and mounding soil)	☐ Loppers (or long-handled pruners)
☐ Japanese weeder	☐ Plant markers
☐ Lawn mower	☐ Spring rake (for leaves)
☐ Secateurs (or hand pruners)	☐ Weeder/edger
☐ Shovel (for hauling)	☐ Wheelbarrow
☐ Spade (for breaking ground)	
☐ Trowel (for planting and weeding)	
☐ Watering hose (with nozzle attachment) or watering can (for patio gardens)	

STRATEGIES

Even experienced gardeners can stand to learn a new trick or two in making the most of their landscapes—patios and windowsills count, too!

1. PLAN YOUR GARDEN

Even small plots should be carefully considered, to reap the biggest rewards.

GROW IN THE ZONE

- For the most part, only grow plants—annuals, perennials, bulbs, shrubs, and trees—that will thrive in your zone (as indicated on the plants' tags); see Gardening Assistance, right, for information.

- If there are plants that you love but are not within your zone, try experimenting on a small scale—annuals and perennials are low-cost investments.

- Zone is less important for vegetables than time to harvest (make sure your season is long enough).

TEST YOUR SOIL

- A soil test will tell you the nature of the earth—acidic versus alkaline, for example—so you can amend it with compost or other fertilizers as needed.

- Fall is a good time to test your soil, as is early spring (before planting); be sure to test your soil at the same time every year.

- You can buy a simple, inexpensive test to perform yourself, or send a sample to your local extension office (see right), which may also advise you on making amendments.

SELECT THE PLANTS

- First identify any existing plantings—you may want to add more of these, or transplant them to a different spot. What has grown well here (or not so much) is also a clue to what you can plant anew.

- Note the amount of sunlight each spot gets during the growing season. "Full sun" plants require six or more hours a day (not necessarily continuous); "partial sun" means four to six hours. There are also plants (hostas, ferns, and bleeding hearts) that do well in light to full shade.

- Extend the season with a variety of plants—from early spring bloomers like daffodils, tulips, and rhododendrons to echinacea, shasta daisies, and hydrangeas that bloom into fall. Astilbe, delphiniums, foxgloves, and peonies fall in between. "Cut and come again" annuals such as cosmos, snapdragons, and zinnias will proliferate all summer long.

- For a vegetable garden, select crops you like to eat or are hard to find. In a limited space, pick plants that grow up, not out, such as beans, tomatoes, and cucumbers. Successive sowing of crops ensures produce all season long, from peas to squashes.

GARDENING ASSISTANCE

When you have questions about what and when to plant (and all other such matters), the Master Gardeners help line at your state university and its local extension offices are there when you need them. Visit the American Horticultural Society (*ahsgardening.org*) for contact information. Or check with the nearest botanical garden or nursery for classes and guidance.

To help you select the plants that prefer your climate, use the Hardiness Zone Map published by the USDA (*planthardiness.ars.usda.gov/PHZMWeb*). Because winter cold is, in most regions, the greatest threat to plant survival, the 13 zones are divided by the annual minimum winter temperature.

MARTHA MUST

When rinsing garden tools with a hose, hold them over a bucket so you can use the water for your flower and vegetable gardens and not waste a drop.

PLOT IT OUT

- Make a blueprint of your yard (or patio), marking where each garden bed, tree, or shrub exists or will go. Note the sun exposure, too.

- It's a good idea to start small; you can plant more shrubs or dig more beds in subsequent years. Plant trees first to allow them time to grow.

- Sketch out your garden bed on graph paper (to scale) to note which plant goes where, keeping in mind the mature size of each plant—as well as any succession plantings. There are also plenty of garden-planning apps and online software out there to help with this task.

- Use twine or plant tags to mark out the plan on the bed—it's all too easy to overcrowd or underutilize your space.

- Plant taller plants, such as the bee balm and black-eyed Susans in the cutting garden at Skylands (shown opposite), where they won't over-shadow shorter plants, like the Bells of Ireland and ageratum here.

2. SHOP THE NURSERY

In addition to ordering from online sources, buying locally allows you to tap into knowledgeable staff as you shop.

WHEN TO GO

- You'll find the most variety at the beginning of the season (particularly spring), depending on where you live.

- Arrive early in the morning for crowd-free shopping—and when staff can better assist you.

- Stop by in the fall when prices are at their lowest—and to get a head start on ordering for the next year.

- Be on the lookout for bargains throughout the year; annuals often go on sale after Memorial Day, for example, and trees and shrubs in midsummer.

WHAT TO BRING

- Take the soil-test results so you can get the right plants (and in case you still need help with amendments).

- Bring your sketches and sunlight recordings, too—many places section plants by "full sun," "partial sun," and "shade."

- Photos of your existing garden and any potential spots will help give the staff a good sense of your space, and allow them to identify your plants.

- Finally, if you have a color palette in mind, include color swatches to help you create a cohesive look.

HOW TO PICK

- Each plant's tag has all the essential information—size, water and sun requirements, bloom period, hardiness zone, and care instructions. Use it to match the plant to the right plot.

- To assess the health of a plant, look for vibrant greenery and abundant shoots. Yellowing, wilting, or scraggly foliage could signal insects or disease.

- Don't be shy about taking a plant out of its pot; it should have hardy roots held in plenty of soil.

- Annuals and flowering perennials should have a few open blooms so you can verify the variety and color.

- Avoid buying flowers, shrubs, and trees that are already blooming—and devoting their energy to reproducing, not root development.

PEST CONTROL

If you're avoiding toxic pesticides—and we all should, for the sake of wildlife, our pets, and our health—try these eco-friendly alternatives:

Let nature run its course by putting ladybugs, lacewings, assassin bugs, and non-stinging parasitic wasps to work in ridding your garden of nuisances. Check with your local nursery or cooperative extension for where to buy them.

Or use this age-old home remedy on outdoor plants (including potted plants and window boxes) to deter aphids and slugs:

1. Purée an onion and two garlic cloves (all peeled), 1 teaspoon cayenne, and 3 cups water in a blender until smooth.

2. Let the mixture sit overnight, then strain the liquid into a spray bottle (it will keep in the refrigerator for two weeks) and use it to coat plants generously every two or three days.

3. PLANT PROPERLY

Give your new plants a healthy start.

PREP THE SOIL

- Seed packets and plant tags provide instructions for planting (depth and spacing, as well as thinning and harvesting for crops). Be sure to save them in a binder with your sketches.

- Most plants do best in loose, well-drained soil, with a lot of organic matter (usually compost) mixed in. Work the soil to a depth of at least 6 inches—deeper for shrubs and trees.

- Add granular fertilizer and water well at time of planting; continue to water frequently for the next couple of weeks.

TIME IT RIGHT

- See page 202 for when to start certain plants from seed (a good idea for crops in areas with short growing seasons); gradually expose seedlings to outdoors over a week to "harden off" before planting in ground.

- Early fall is the best time to plant spring-blooming bulbs, next year's perennials (or to divide and replant existing ones), and even trees and shrubs—this allows you to also devote your spring gardening to other tasks. Plant while the ground is still warm, at least six weeks before the first hard frost.

- Otherwise (and always for annuals and seedlings) wait for spring, when the ground has warmed to at least 55°F and after the last frost; summer bloomers can be planted later in milder climates.

- Crops can—and should, in the case of succession planting— be planted all season long in a vegetable garden.

4. NURTURE PLANTS

Learning when and how to feed, water, and weed gets easier with practice.

FEED AND WATER

- Fertilize all plants and beds in early spring— or the date of the last frost in colder regions; trees and shrubs can have another light feeding in late fall. Roses require their own upkeep (check the care label). Water well after feeding.

- Apply a deep layer of mulch in early spring or later in the fall to keep the soil moist and prevent weeds.

- Flowers and shrubs need 1 to 2 inches of water per week (more for container plants). Water early in the morning (the best time) or late afternoon. Get a rain gauge to help with measuring.

MARTHA MUST

At my Skylands home in Maine, I gather moss, lichens, and ferns from the property to create miniature "forests" for keeping indoors, layering crushed gravel in rustic containers and arranging my finds to mimic nature. When the plants begin fading, I return them to their rightful place and replace them with others.

WEED AND PRUNE

- Young weeds can be pulled out with your hands; for those with deep taproots, like dandelions, use a hori hori to dig down and remove the entire plant, roots and all. Weed after a rain or water first, to ease the job.

- To quickly get rid of a trouble spot, pour boiling water or white vinegar over it (but not on grass); repeat as needed.

- Always dispose of weeds in your regular trash, where they can't proliferate.

- Deadhead flowering plants to encourage new growth, either by pinching off spent blooms or cutting stems to an inch above their bases; leave foliage to gather energy for next year's growth, removing any brown foliage before it drops and turns to rot (attracting pests).

- Spring-flowering blooms should be pruned right after they're done flowering; roses should also be pruned after blooming.

- Some summer-flowering shrubs bloom on old growth while others on new, so ask your local garden center how to prune your specific specimen.

5. GROW HOUSEPLANTS

Besides being lovely to look at, houseplants help purify the air. Grow them with the following in mind.

CHOOSE

- Succulents and cacti are practically foolproof—just several hours of sun and not too much water.

- Other low-maintenance options include philodendron, ZZ plant, dieffenbachia, begonia, and aloe.

WATER

- Some plants need twice-daily watering, others once a month (whenever the top 2 inches of soil feel dry).

- Aim for the soil. Use a small watering can with a long, slender spout to avoid getting foliage wet.

- A mister works well on ferns and other plants, especially during the winter when heating can leave the foliage parched.

- If your plant is showing signs of overwatering (yellow, wilted leaves), let it dry out between waterings.

- Before going on a short vacation, cluster your plants together, away from the light—even sun-loving varieties. That way, they won't dry out as quickly. If you're away for more

LONGER-LASTING BOUQUETS

To make the most of your cutting-garden flower arrangements:

1. Trim the stems with gardening shears at a 45-degree angle so the flowers can take in more water.
2. For woody branches such as lilacs, cut an asterisk in the base or crush the last few inches of the branch with a hammer or mallet.
3. Be sure to strip leaves that would otherwise sit below the waterline.
4. Fill the vase with lukewarm water, and add a generous pinch of oxygen bleach.
5. Arrange the bouquet, and set it in a cool spot out of direct sunlight.
6. Every couple of days, change the water, and re-clip the stems.

than a week, though, you'll need to get a plant sitter.

FERTILIZE

- Most houseplants need fertilizing from March through September.

- Fertilize both leafy and flowering plants once every two weeks; the same goes for plants that flower during the winter, including after blooming.

- Always dampen the soil before feeding so the nutrients go where needed.

CLEAN

- Dust and oils block sunlight, so clean plant leaves at least once a month.

- Spray succulents and cacti with compressed air or dust with a soft brush (water will cause leaf rot).

- For other plants: Wipe smooth leaves with a damp bar towel or rag; lightly mist others.

- To clean several plants at once, set them in the shower under a fine, tepid spray. Then blot excess moisture.

CONTROL PESTS

- Check often—such as when watering—for signs of infestation.

- Brush leaves with a cotton swab dipped in alcohol to get rid of any insects.

- Regular cleaning will also help—you can add a few drops of all-natural insecticidal soap (such as neem oil) to the water.

REPOT

- If you notice roots peeking through the pot's holes, soil drying out too quickly, or that the leaves and stems have stopped growing, the plant may be pot-bound and needs a larger container.

REVIVE

- Even if a houseplant doesn't need repotting, you should still replenish its soil once a year. Use a fork to remove the top 2 to 4 inches, taking care not to harm the roots. Replace with fresh potting soil.

- A distressed plant might express it in a number of ways: Look for leaves turning pale, or frequent wilting.

- Rotate plants a quarter turn every other week (or when it is leaning toward the light) for even growth.

- Experiment with watering and sun exposure until you find the right fit.

- If your houseplant just doesn't seem happy, try starting all over again with a healthy cutting.

WINTERIZE

- During the cold season, try not to disturb plants by relocating or repotting them.

- Let up on watering and fertilizing, too.

- Resume your regular routine once daylight hours extend and growth resurges.

6. CARE FOR THE LAWN

Care tips depend on the type of grass and your climate, but here is some general guidance.

MOW

- Wait until grass is at least 2 inches tall before mowing—and never cut off more than the top third.

- Mow when the grass is dry, preferably in the afternoon or early evening.

- Use a string trimmer for hard-to-reach spots.

WATER

- A lawn needs, on average, an inch per week, climate depending.

- Water deeply once or twice a week in the morning.

- A soaker hose or pulsing sprinkler will send moisture straight to the roots where it's needed.

- In drought-prone areas, consider replacing your lawn with drought-tolerant plants to conserve water.

FERTILIZE

- Feed the lawn in early spring and again in late summer (if necessary).

- Use organic products (chemicals harm wildlife).

- Seed bare spots in spring, once the temperature reaches 65°F.

MARTHA MUST

Ease the dirty work of potting plants indoors by employing a broad, shallow bin as a portable potting bench (no more newspaper-covered surfaces). You can do all your fertilizing and repotting within its confines, containing any mess. Afterward, dump the excess dirt, then store supplies (extra pots, stakes, potting mix, gravel) right inside.

ANNUAL SCHEDULE

In some parts of the country, gardening season is a year-round undertaking. Where you live will determine how often you'll need to get certain tasks done.

ONCE OR TWICE A DAY

☐ Clean your tools at the end of each day's use.

☐ Water outdoor potted plants, including hanging baskets and window boxes.

ONCE OR TWICE A WEEK

☐ Mow the lawn.

☐ Check for fading flowers, and deadhead.

☐ Remove spent annuals from garden bed, as needed.

☐ Harvest fresh herbs.

☐ Stay on top of weeds!

☐ Water garden beds and lawn (or more as needed).

☐ Fertilize and water houseplants (or as needed); check for pests.

ONCE OR TWICE A MONTH

☐ Clean and sharpen lawn edger (especially if you use it often).

☐ Rotate houseplants a quarter turn.

☐ Clean houseplants.

ONCE OR TWICE A SEASON

☐ Sharpen and oil garden tools.

☐ Fertilize trees, shrubs, and garden beds.

☐ Prune perennials and shrubs.

ONCE OR TWICE A YEAR

☐ Repot houseplants, or replenish with new potting soil.

☐ Organize potting supplies.

☐ Service lawn mower and weeder.

☐ Seed and aerate lawn.

☐ Use spade to edge garden beds (keeping grass from migrating in and mulch from washing out).

☐ Fertilize the lawn.

☐ Prune trees.

☐ Divide and plant perennials.

☐ Mulch garden beds and around trees and shrubs.

PLANTING VEGETABLES

Many crops—peas, green beans, carrots, radishes, spinach, lettuces, cucumbers, and squashes—can be direct-sown as soon as the soil has warmed (meaning always in more temperate regions, where you can grow the vegetables listed below in the ground, too). In northern regions, the following crops fare better when started as seeds indoors, as specified before the date of the last frost.

8 to 12 weeks before: Eggplants, artichokes, celery, and onions.

4 to 8 weeks before: Cabbage, cauliflower, broccoli, kale, brussels sprouts, and tomatoes.

SEASONAL SCHEDULE

Of all areas of home organization, caring for the lawn and garden is most tied to the seasons; adapt the checklist below to your own conditions.

WINTER

- [ ] Scale back on watering and fertilizing houseplants; prune to keep new growth in check (to preserve nutrients).
- [ ] Draft planting plan for spring garden.
- [ ] Prune damaged trees; keep on the lookout.
- [ ] Prune fruit trees (after coldest weather has passed).
- [ ] Order seeds.
- [ ] Have mower and edger serviced.
- [ ] Sharpen and oil garden tools.
- [ ] Buy plant labels and markers (and also reuse what you have).

SPRING

- [ ] Remove winter plant coverings.
- [ ] Edge driveway and garden beds.
- [ ] Rake leaves; compost.
- [ ] Hook up garden hose.
- [ ] Organize potting supplies.
- [ ] For lawns, fertilize cool-season grass in early spring; seed warm-season grass later in season.
- [ ] Begin fertilizing beds, trees, and shrubs (as well as houseplants).
- [ ] Repot houseplants as needed.
- [ ] Begin mowing and watering lawn.
- [ ] Direct-sow or start seeds indoors for crops (see opposite); plant rhubarb and potatoes.
- [ ] Direct-sow seeds for spring vegetables.
- [ ] Plant new trees.
- [ ] Plant window boxes and hanging baskets.
- [ ] Set up peony supports.
- [ ] Buy and plant summer-blooming bulbs and shrubs.
- [ ] Plant bush and pole beans.
- [ ] Set out and stake tomatoes, eggplants, and peppers.

SUMMER

- [ ] Finish planting perennial beds (before heat sets in).
- [ ] Deadhead perennials (as needed).
- [ ] Stop fertilizing lawn, shrubs, and beds before end of summer.
- [ ] Plant sunflowers (and other late-summer and fall annuals).
- [ ] Order bulbs for fall planting (depending on your zone).
- [ ] For a fall harvest, plant crucifers, such as brussels sprouts, cabbage, and broccoli.
- [ ] Harvest crops.

FALL

- [ ] After last mowing, clean mower and edger thoroughly; empty gas tank.
- [ ] Plant cool-weather greens.
- [ ] Pick last-of-season tomatoes and herbs.
- [ ] Pull faded annuals from flower beds.
- [ ] Buy and plant spring-blooming bulbs; dig up and store more delicate bulbs, like dahlias.
- [ ] Divide and plant summer-blooming perennials (or wait until spring if it has been a rainy fall).
- [ ] Plant new trees.
- [ ] Seed cool-season lawns.
- [ ] Cut back perennials.
- [ ] Have your sprinkler system drained and serviced, and flag any heads near driveways or walkways to prevent damage during snow removal.
- [ ] Rake fall leaves and use as mulch or in compost.
- [ ] Cover boxwoods and other shrubs with burlap, if desired. Add compost and mulch to cut-back perennials for winter protection.

HOME

When it comes to home upkeep, it seems there is always something that requires our attention. Of course, the amount of routine maintenance—to keep your space looking its best and head off costly fixes—depends on the dwelling (an apartment presents fewer plumbing, heating, and exterior tasks than a spacious colonial, for instance). But in every case, you'll need a checklist and season-by-season schedule so you can stay organized— plus some handy know-how for tackling it all with ease.

COOK

Cooking is so much more than following a recipe—though that's certainly part of it. The best and most efficient home cooking involves thoughtful meal planning, a smart shopping strategy, and the right storage methods to keep your food fresh. It also calls for getting creative, with flavor combinations as well as with meals for every occasion, from leisurely Sunday breakfasts to box lunches to quick-but-healthy weeknight dinners. Read on for kitchen-tested strategies by the dozen.

SUPPLIES

Every home cook needs three knives: a chef's knife, a paring knife, and a serrated knife. Start with those, and the other essentials below, then add specialized tools as needed.

ESSENTIALS	EXTRAS
☐ Baking sheets (rimmed and flat)	☐ Bench scraper
☐ Bar towels	☐ Blender (regular or immersion)
☐ Box grater	☐ Citrus press
☐ Can opener	☐ Food processor (or mini chopper)
☐ Cutting boards	☐ Kitchen tongs
☐ Electric mixer	☐ Rasp-style grater
☐ Flexible spatulas	☐ Spice grinder (or mortar and pestle)
☐ Knives: chef's knife or Japanese cleaver, paring knife, serrated knife	☐ Vegetable peeler
☐ Measuring cups and spoons	
☐ Metal slotted spoon and spatula	
☐ Pots and pans: cast-iron skillet, sauté pan, stockpot, and saucepans	
☐ Wooden spoons	

STRATEGIES

With a smart selection of foundational and flavor-building ingredients on hand, easy meals are always within reach. Other efficiency-boosting lessons are here for the borrowing, too.

1. STOCK THE PANTRY

Think of your pantry as your arsenal, not a place to stockpile. When preparing dishes with only a few ingredients, quality is key.

BEANS AND LEGUMES

Buy and store: Buy dried beans in bulk; decant them into storage containers; look for BPA-free and low-sodium canned products.

Pro tip: To quick-soak dried beans (rather than overnight), cover them in a large pot with water and bring to a boil; turn off heat, cover, and let stand for an hour. Drain off soaking water before cooking beans on their own or in soups and stews.

CANNED TOMATOES

Buy and store: Choose whole peeled tomatoes over crushed or diced, for fresher flavor. Tomato paste adds umami to soups, stews, and sauces.

Pro tip: Snip whole tomatoes (still in the can) with kitchen shears before using in cooking; to make crushed tomatoes, purée them with an immersion blender until coarse.

DRIED HERBS AND SPICES

Buy and store: Buy whole, when possible, in small quantities and grind as needed. Keep herbs in a cool, dark spot and replace when they lose their aroma.

Pro tip: Toast spices in a dry skillet to bring out their aromatic oils before using in sweet and savory preparations.

NUTS AND SEEDS

Buy and store: Keep some at room temperature for using within a few months and freeze the rest for a year or more.

Pro tip: Use a surplus to make nut (or seed) butters: Purée in a food processor with salt and spices to taste and to desired consistency; refrigerate up to six months.

OILS AND VINEGARS

Buy and store: Extra-virgin olive oil (for vinaigrettes, drizzling, and low-heat cooking), coconut oil (for baking and roasting), and safflower oil (for high-heat stove-top cooking) will cover your needs; vinegars (red-wine, balsamic or sherry vinegar, and apple cider) are used for dressings and sauces. Keep oils and vinegars away from heat or sunlight.

Pro tip: Toasted sesame oil also adds depth to vinaigrettes and when drizzled over soups and stir-fries and noodle dishes.

WHOLE GRAINS

Buy and store: Buy oats, barley, farro, and others in bulk. Decant into storage containers (tape cooking instructions inside lid).

Pro tip: Toasting grains in a little oil before adding the cooking liquid imparts extra flavor to the dish.

TINNED FISH

Buy and store: Look for oil-packed (and wild-caught) sardines, tuna, salmon, and mackerel. Once opened, refrigerate in an airtight container for three days.

Pro tip: Sockeye or "red salmon" is meatier than the standard pink variety; "regular" (vs. "premium") contains the skin and soft, edible bones, for optimum omega-3s and calcium.

STOCKS AND BROTHS

Buy and store: Look for low-sodium varieties from a carton—or make your own (page 19).

Pro tip: Boost store-bought broth by simmering it for a half hour with vegetable scraps, kombu strips, or a little miso.

FAVORITE FLAVOR BUILDERS

Count on these ingredients to give your dishes more depth.

Anchovies: Forget their fishy reputation. Just a bit of this tiny cured fish can bring a big umami flavor boost to pastas, soups, sauces, and salad dressings.

Capers: Fold the salt-packed variety into egg, tuna, and potato salad as well as cream cheese (for bagels); roast with cauliflower (and raisins, Sicilian-style); or fry and use as a garnish for seafood and green salads.

Curry paste: Besides being a flavor base for curries and stir-fries, Thai-style pastes can be mixed into mayonnaise for a sandwich spread or a dip for crudités.

Dijon mustard: A must for vinaigrettes, marinades, sauces, and glazes—and when breading cutlets (it goes on first).

Harissa: Spread this North African chile paste on a grilled cheese or spoon it into soups or tagines before serving.

Parmesan cheese: Grate or shave Parmigiano-Reggiano over pasta, risotto, and so many other Italian-style dishes—and add the rinds to broths and soups for incomparable taste.

Preserved lemons: These fermented fruits get better with age, adding punch to pastas, tagines, roast chicken, grain salads, and salsas and dips.

Tahini: It's not just for hummus—this sesame-seed paste tastes great in salad dressings and is a quick base for sesame noodles.

Worcestershire sauce: Try this condiment to add depth and salty sweetness to marinades, salad dressings (a drop will do), sauces, and Bloody Marys.

2. PLAN MEALS FOR THE WEEK

Cooking the majority of your meals will do you (and your budget) good.

CALENDAR IT IN

Spend an hour over the weekend perusing your go-to sources for inspiration and plotting out meals. Aim to add at least one new dish to your regular rotation every week—updating a longtime favorite also counts.

START WITH WHAT YOU HAVE

Take inventory of your foodstuffs—it's easy to lose sight of items you come across every day (or when they've been pushed to the back of the shelf). Plan meals around anything that's approaching its end date, including eggs, dairy, and produce in the refrigerator.

WORK IN SEASONAL PRODUCE

Eating what's fresh will always result in the best-tasting and most nutritious meals. The more local, the better—scour the specialty grocers and supermarket for "local" signs, visit the farmers' market, and/or sign up for a weekly CSA share. Use foods that perish most easily early in the week. Also, put trimmings to use—broccoli and cauliflower stalks and leaves can be eaten raw (shaved into salads) or roasted (just like the florets).

STRETCH INGREDIENTS

Account for a surplus by incorporating them into more than one meal. Cilantro, for example, can be in Monday's dinner and also Wednesday's breakfast scramble (or make pesto, page 54); save extra rice from Tuesday's dinner for the next day's lunch salad or fried-rice supper; add leftover buttermilk to your morning smoothie.

3. STREAMLINE THE SHOPPING

The goals: fewer trips to the market, getting the most value from your dollar, and avoiding waste.

MAKE A LIST

After you've decided on your weekly menu, jot down all the ingredients (on paper or digitally) you need to shop for; some meal-plan apps generate a list for you. It helps to organize the items to match the store's layout—with produce, dairy, grains, oils and vinegars, and so on grouped together—so you can easily tick off the boxes as you go and avoid overlooking anything.

SHOP FOR THE FREEZER

Take advantage of "two-for-one" or other discounts on bacon, sausage, butter, flour, cornmeal, hard (not soft) cheese, bread, and milk (dairy and otherwise)—all of which can be frozen and used later.

GO GREEN

Bring along your own washable totes, preferably made from natural fibers. Unless your store has compostable ones, skip the bags and put produce directly in your tote (you're going to wash those greens anyway)—or bring your own fabric bags.

4. PREP AHEAD THE PRODUCE

Rather than immediately putting vegetables in the refrigerator (only to forget about them), prep them right out of the shopping tote or CSA box. You'll save valuable refrigerator space—and be more inclined to use your purchases. The same idea goes for prepping produce the night before or morning of, so dinner is that much quicker to prepare.

AROMATICS

Garlic: Peel cloves and keep in a jar with a tight-fitting lid; they'll stay fresh for a week or longer. Mince or slice when ready to use.

Onion, shallot, and scallions: These are best when chopped or sliced only a few hours—or up to overnight—before using. Seal tightly (and double-bag them) to keep your refrigerator from smelling like onions.

Fresh ginger: Peel (with a spoon), wrap in plastic, and freeze in a resealable bag for six months (no need to thaw before grating or slicing).

ASPARAGUS

Snap off tough stems and stand, tips up, in a glass with a couple inches of water; they will stay crisp for two or three days longer in the refrigerator.

BELL PEPPERS

Trim to remove stem, ribs, and seeds; chop or cut flesh into strips, or leave whole or halved for stuffing; refrigerate in an airtight container for two or three days.

TIP

When storing prepped (diced or sliced) produce in a plastic bag or airtight container, wrap it in or top with a damp paper towel to keep the items fresher longer.

CABBAGE (RED, GREEN, NAPA, SAVOY)

Halve head through stem, then trim and remove outer leaves; chop, slice, or shred leaves and keep in an airtight container for one or two days.

CELERY

Rinse, dry, and chop or slice stalks and keep in an airtight container for a week or two; save the tender inner leaves in a separate bag for salads and garnishes.

CRUCIFERS (BROCCOLI AND CAULIFLOWER)

Separate head into florets; peel stalk and cut into pieces. Refrigerate separately in airtight containers. Use within a week.

FENNEL

Trim stalks and reserve frilly fronds in a plastic or paper bag (add to salads, pasta, and soups); chop or slice bulb and keep in an airtight container, wrapped in a damp paper towel (or rub with a cut lemon), for two to three days.

FRESH HERBS (MINT, CILANTRO, PARSLEY, BASIL, ROSEMARY, THYME)

If using within a few days, store washed and dried herbs in a plastic bag in the refrigerator. To make them last longer, trim an inch from stems and stand bunches upright in a glass or jar with a couple inches of water; secure a plastic bag over the top. Leave on the counter where you can snip off what you need as you go; change the water after a week (the herbs will keep for another week).

LEAFY GREENS (KALE, COLLARDS, SWISS CHARD, SPINACH)

Strip leaves from tough stems, then wash and dry and cut into ribbons or tear into bite-size pieces; refrigerate in a plastic bag (saving chard stems and storing them separately for sautéing). These greens will keep for as long as a week; you can revive them with a quick stint in an ice-water bath (same for lettuces).

LEGUMES (GREEN BEANS, SNAP PEAS, SNOW PEAS)

Rinse and dry, then snap stem end to remove, and pull off strings; keep beans or peas in a plastic bag in the vegetable drawer up to two or three days.

LETTUCES (ROMAINE, RED OR GREEN LEAF, MÂCHE, BOSTON/BIBB)

Separate leaves, wash and gently spin-dry, then store in a plastic bag in the crisper drawer for a few days (or as long as leaves appear fresh). Wait until ready to serve to tear or cut into bite-size pieces.

ROOT VEGETABLES (CARROTS, RADISHES, TURNIPS, PARSNIPS, BEETS)

Remove any intact tops right away, leaving an inch attached; wash and dry tops, then refrigerate in plastic bags for a day. Beet and turnip greens are good sautéed with garlic, while radish and carrot tops can be added to salads.

- You can peel and chop, slice, or grate carrots, turnips, and parsnips; refrigerate in an airtight container for two or three days.

- Soak radishes to remove dirt and grit, then drain on paper towels before refrigerating, three or four days.

- Beets are easier to peel after cooking, so just scrub them well; refrigerated, they'll last at least a week.

SUMMER SQUASHES AND ZUCCHINI

Slice, chop, or shred up to three days ahead; refrigerate in an airtight container.

WINTER SQUASHES (BUTTERNUT, ACORN, KABOCHA)

If you plan to eat it within a few days, cut squash into slices or cubes (peel butternut; kabocha and acorn squashes have edible skins) and keep in an airtight container in the refrigerator.

MARTHA MUST

When I will be using butternut squash in a soup or pie filling, I like to roast the whole (unpeeled) squash for deeper flavor on a rimmed baking sheet at 425°F for about 45 minutes or until very tender when pierced with a knife; when cool, peel off the skin and discard the seeds, then put the flesh in an airtight container and refrigerate for a week or freeze for up to three months.

5. DO BIG-BATCH COOKING

Over the weekend, make these jump-start components for weekday meals.

COOKED BEANS AND LENTILS

Once the beans are cooked, drained, and cooled, transfer them to single-serve freezer bags, pressing out excess air. Drop frozen beans into a pan of simmering water to heat through, or add (frozen) beans to stews and casseroles at the start.

COOKED GRAINS

Keep extra grains in freezer bags, pressing them flat (let cool before storing). Break off pieces to put in soup, or reheat portions for your breakfast, lunch, or dinner "bowls."

CASSEROLES

Shop for twice the ingredients and assemble two dishes (lasagna or enchiladas, for example); bake one for serving that night and freeze the other one for another week.

ROAST MEATS

A whole chicken isn't the only candidate for make-ahead meat. Try pork loin or turkey breast as well. Shred meat and use in tacos or enchilada fillings, pasta dishes, stir-fries, ramen dishes, even salads. Refrigerate the meat in an airtight container up to four days.

ROAST VEGETABLES

Roast broccoli, cauliflower, brussels sprouts, potatoes, squashes, or other vegetables on Sunday, refrigerate in airtight containers, and eat them with grains, beans, pasta, or salads—or as a side—all week.

SOUPS AND STEWS

Put your slow cooker or stockpot to work, churning out hearty one-dish meals. Divide these into portions (for one, two, or four servings) instead of freezing the whole dish; they will keep up to six months. (See page 66 for how to make any soup.)

6. PRESERVE THE SEASON

Extend the summer-to-fall harvest for months to come using one of the following methods.

FREEZE

Done properly, many fruits, vegetables, and herbs can be frozen for as long as six months without compromising their taste and texture.

■ To prevent clumping, first spread fruits or vegetables in a single layer on a rimmed baking sheet before freezing. Once the produce is firm (after about an hour), transfer to resealable bags, label, and freeze.

■ Freeze whole berries and pitted cherries; cut pitted plums, peaches, nectarines, apricots, and mangoes into slices (toss with 1,000 milligrams ascorbic acid or a crushed vitamin C tablet for every pound of fruit to prevent browning). Citrus can be peeled and segmented, bananas peeled and left whole or cut into chunks.

■ Tomatoes, sliced bell peppers, mushrooms, and corn kernels can be frozen as is, but green beans, okra, summer squashes and zucchini, and eggplant should first be blanched for three minutes, then

plunged into an ice-water bath (to stop the cooking) and drained well; then cut beans in half and okra into pieces, if desired.

■ Chop a bunch of fresh basil, mint, parsley, or cilantro, mix with a splash of olive oil, and pour into an ice-cube tray; once solid, pop the cubes into resealable bags and freeze for three months.

QUICK-PICKLE

Start with best-quality produce, and wash it well. (Run your containers through the dishwasher's hot-water cycle before you begin.) Use these "refrigerator" pickles to perk up burgers, sandwiches, and cheese platters.

Basic Formula

Try pickling anything you've got a glut of, such as zucchini, tomatoes, corn, green beans, wax beans, cherry peppers, okra, or peaches; unripe produce, including green tomatoes and green strawberries; and even watermelon rinds that might otherwise be discarded.

1. Make the brine: Combine 1½ cups distilled white vinegar or apple-cider vinegar, ¾ cup water (½ cup for cucumbers), 2 teaspoons sugar, 2 tablespoons whole spices (such as peppercorns, juniper

MARTHA MUST

Every summer I make jam from fresh apricots. When simmering the fruit, I include five or six of the pits to add depth of flavor, then remove them before ladling the jam into jars.

berries, coriander seeds, mustard seeds), 1 or 2 bay leaves, and 2 tablespoons coarse salt in a saucepan. Bring to a boil, stirring until sugar and salt are dissolved.

2. Make pickles: Pack clean jars or airtight containers firmly with vegetables or fruit. Add boiling brine to cover completely. Let cool. Cover and refrigerate at least 1 week or up to 3 months before serving.

Variations

Besides the flavor pairings below, experiment with different vinegars—sherry or red- or white-wine vinegar will all work.

Cherry Tomatoes:

4 cups very small cherry or grape tomatoes, plus 2 small sprigs rosemary

Chile Cauliflower:

4 cups small cauliflower florets (halve or quarter larger ones), 2 small fresh red chiles, and 4 sprigs thyme

Dilly Beets: 12 ounces baby beets, peeled and cut into ½-inch wedges, plus 8 sprigs dill and 4 cloves garlic; add beets to brine with spices in step 1

Dill Cucumbers:

1 pound Kirby cucumbers, trimmed and cut into wedges, plus 8 sprigs dill and 4 cloves garlic

Onions and Peppers:

2 small red onions, 8 baby bell peppers, and 1 small jalapeño, all cut into rings

Radishes: 4 cups very small radishes, trimmed and larger ones halved

MAKE JAM

Turn out jars of freezer jam throughout the summer so you can enjoy pick-of-season flavor long after fruit disappears from farmstands—and all without standing over a steaming pot on the stove.

Basic Formula

This streamlined formula works well for ripe summer fruit—plums, peaches, nectarines, strawberries, blueberries, raspberries, and blackberries.

1. Stir together 3 pounds berries or stone fruit (cut into 1-inch chunks), 1½ pounds sugar (3⅓ cups), and ¼ teaspoon salt in a large heavy-bottomed pot. Bring to a boil, stirring

until sugar is dissolved and mashing fruit with a potato masher (or a large spoon).

2. Add 2 tablespoons fresh lemon juice; continue to boil, stirring frequently, until bubbles slow, chunks of fruit show at top, and mixture clings to a spoon (it will still fall off in clumps), 10 to 12 minutes. Skim foam from top.

3. Ladle jam into clean jars or containers, leaving ¾ inch of headroom. Let cool completely. Cover and refrigerate up to 1 month or freeze up to 1 year.

Variations

The skins from stone fruit lend pretty color and more flavor to the jam; for a smoother texture, peel peaches or nectarines: Carve an X in the bottom of each and plunge them into boiling water for 30 seconds, then transfer fruit to an ice-water bath; the skins will slip off. For plums, just lift the skins out of the cooked jam with a fork.

Mixed Berry: 1 pound raspberries, blackberries or blueberries, and strawberries

Nectarine-Raspberry: 2¼ pounds nectarines plus 12 ounces raspberries

Peach-Plum: 1½ pounds each peaches and plums

SCHEDULE

Organizing your cooking routine boils down to putting meal planning on the front burner—and having a seasonal slant to your shopping and recipe selection.

DAILY

- [ ] Prep for the next day's meals.

WEEKLY

- [ ] Plan meals and snacks for the week ahead; make a shopping list (with the goal of shopping for the bulk of the ingredients in one trip).
- [ ] Check perishables and replace as needed.
- [ ] Shop for ingredients, using the list from the weekly meal plan.
- [ ] Shop the farmers' market; pick up CSA share.

If you have 5 minutes...
- Rearrange the spice (or other) drawer.
- Purge the refrigerator.

If you have 10 minutes...
- Do next-day meal prep.
- Explore new recipes.

If you have 15 minutes...
- Go through freezer; make a plan to use items near their end date.

- [ ] Prep ahead over the weekend, using the strategies on pages 218 to 221.
- [ ] Explore cookbooks and online sites for new recipes to avoid the rotation rut.

MONTHLY

- [ ] Focus on in-season fruits and vegetables (see monthly In-Season Picks in Part One).
- [ ] Prepare and use freeze-ahead meals.

SEASONALLY

- [ ] Rotate cookbooks and cooking equipment (swapping the slow cooker for grilling tools, for example).
- [ ] Preserve summer produce by freezing it or making quick pickles and jams.
- [ ] Sharpen knives.

TWICE YEARLY

- [ ] Purge the pantry, tossing out expired items.
- [ ] Take inventory of cooking tools and equipment and replace as needed.

COOKING BY TIMETABLE

Figuring out a way to share a homemade dinner with your family is all about cooking when it works for you.

The Weekend Cook: You don't have time to cook every weeknight, and you'd like people to fix their own meals when you're not home.

The Plan: Invest a few hours on a weekend to prep multiple meals. Make hearty soups (page 66) and casseroles, and measure out serving amounts before freezing.

The A.M. Cook: You have more time in the morning than the evening, and you prefer to have a ready-to-go meal in the refrigerator to allow for flexible eating schedules.

The Plan: Prepare easy meals before breakfast, focusing on dishes that take 45 minutes or less and reheat well—think meatloaf rather than steak, sautéed chicken thighs rather than grilled breasts. Frittatas and pasta salads taste great cold or at room temperature.

The Short-Order Cook: Making dinner is a top priority for you, as is keeping a well-stocked kitchen. Rather than sticking to a recipe, you buy what looks good and is well-priced at the store.

The Plan: Do a big shop on the weekend for mix-and-match ingredients: quick-cooking proteins (cutlets, steaks, sausages, and tofu) and vegetables, plus canned tomatoes and beans and assorted grains and pasta.

ENTERTAIN

Think of the most relaxed and gracious party host you know. What's the key to her success? Being organized probably has a lot to do with it. Advance planning is what makes any size social gathering go smoothly. And of course, many other fundamental lessons in this book— sticking to a cleaning schedule, keeping the kitchen well stocked—also take the pressure off.

SUPPLIES

Keep it simple—your everyday dishes, flatware, and glasses will do. Save the splurge-worthy additions for multipurpose items, like boards, platters, and pitchers.

ESSENTIALS	EXTRAS
☐ Attractive flatware (buy lots at tag sales and flea markets)	☐ Candles and votives
☐ Cloth napkins	☐ Chargers (they can also be used as trays)
☐ Cups and saucers (for after-dinner coffee and tea)	☐ Large wood cutting board (for prepping and serving, such as for a cheese platter)
☐ Glassware (page 231)	☐ Pitchers and/or carafes
☐ Salad and dinner plates (neutrals are the most versatile, and they don't all have to match)	☐ Vases and other vessels (for displaying flowers from guests or your own garden)
☐ Serving platter (at least one large one, more as desired)	☐ Wooden salad bowl
☐ Wide, shallow bowls (for soups, stews, risotto, and more)	

STRATEGIES

For casual get-togethers you can play it loose, without a lot of planning. For everything else, though, your advance work will pay off in a party that goes off without a hitch.

1. STOCK THE KITCHEN

Start with the everyday staples on page 215 and flavor boosters on page 217 (some are repeated below, for emphasis). Then all that's left is to pick up fresh items (fruit and cheese, for example) for quick and easy nibbles.

- Assorted mustards, like Dijon, grainy, horseradish, honey-mustard, etc.

- Jams (page 223), chutneys, and fruit pastes (such as membrillo)

- Honey (for drizzling over cheese and fruit)

- Dried apricots, figs, dates, and other fruits

- Pickles (page 223) and caper berries

- Piquillo peppers and pepperoncini

- Jarred salsas (in a pinch) and canned chipotles

- A variety of nuts (kept in the freezer), including plain and seasoned (tamari almonds, curried cashews) and shell-on pistachios

- Wasabi peas, seaweed sheets, rice crackers, and sesame sticks

- Dried salami and other shelf-stable meats

- Chips, crackers, and crispbreads (including some gluten-free options)

- Corn tortillas and pita breads (freeze for longer storage)

- Popcorn kernels (and favorite seasonings)

- Canned beans (for easy dips or making roasted chickpeas)

- Tinned fish (for toast and salad toppers)

- Sea salts, dried chiles, and other seasonings (such as za'atar or Aleppo pepper)

- High-quality chocolate bars, biscotti, and Danish biscuits

- Puff pastry and phyllo dough (in the freezer)

2. CURATE THE HOME BAR

Whether yours is a rolling cart (page 130) or a full wet bar, here's what to stock it with.

BUY THE BASIC TOOLS
You don't need a lot of equipment to mix a cocktail. Start with these supplies and then branch out as you expand your repertoire, or if you tend to host a lot of gatherings.

- Bottle opener and corkscrew

- Cocktail shaker and strainer

- Jigger (with a 1-ounce and ¾-ounce measure)

- Muddler (or the handle of a wooden spoon)

- Bar spoon

- Citrus peeler and press

- Ice bucket and tongs plus ice-cube trays

GO EASY ON GLASSWARE

Unless you routinely throw huge parties, six to eight glasses in each basic style is fine (you can always rent extras for that holiday bash!): an all-purpose wineglass (with stems or without, or even a European-style tumbler), or, if you prefer, separate red and white; highball and rocks glasses; plus champagne flutes.

DON'T OVERTHINK THE DRINKS

- Have at least one red, a white, and maybe a rosé or sparkling wine; a pale lager or an amber ale is a safe bet for beer drinkers. Buying these by the mix-and-match case is more economical than individual bottles or six-packs.

- Because spirits won't last forever (typically one to two years), there's no sense in overspending. Vodka, gin, tequila, rum (light or dark), bourbon, and scotch are the mainstays, but you need not have them all or all the time. Same for vermouth and other liqueurs. Instead, store only what you like to drink and pick up others when the occasion calls for it.

- Another way to edit your purchases is to focus them on a few signature cocktails—experimenting is all part of the fun. Jot down or print out the recipe so guests can help themselves.

- For mixers or nonalcoholic refreshers, go beyond club soda, tonic water, and fruit juices and shop for small-batch sodas, ginger beer, shrubs (or "drinking vinegars"), and kombucha.

GO BIG ON GARNISHES

Citrus, olives, caper berries, cocktail onions, maraschino cherries, pickled anything, fresh herbs, and even peppercorns or juniper berries are long-lasting and easy to keep in steady supply.

3. CREATE A CACHE OF GO-TO RECIPES

It's a good idea to develop a roster of favorites (and to find make-ahead options; see right), working new ones into the rotation over time.

STARTERS

- These could be as simple as a big bowl of seasoned popcorn or spiced nuts.

- Satays and skewers with sauces for dipping make great finger foods, cooked either on the grill or under the broiler.

- Cheese boards or charcuterie platters make beautiful presentations and prove satisfying. Keep all the accoutrements in the larder (page 47), then pick up fruit, soft cheeses, meats, and other fresh options.

- Mezze and antipasti spreads are in a similar vein. Round out store-bought items with a couple homemade offerings, such as baba ghanoush and hummus, or marinated peppers and grilled vegetables, respectively.

MAIN COURSES

- Robust one-pot meals such as chili, pozole, caldo verde, and curries offer warm satisfaction in cooler months. Plus, it's fun for guests to pick and choose from the usual toppings.

- Oven-to-table braises and tagines afford hands-off cooking, letting you focus on other things; you can even prepare these a day ahead and reheat them before your guests arrive.

- Risotto and paella are both classics that never go out of style. They're endlessly adaptable, too—especially when hosting vegetarian guests.

PARTY MAKE-AHEADS

Load the menu with items that can be prepared, at least partially, in advance.

- Opt for dips and spreads that can be refrigerated for a day or so—or can be baked after freezing.

- Gougères, cheese straws, and other savory pastries—mini quiches included—are freeze-and-bake bites.

- Braises and stews taste even better the next day—or put your slow cooker to work the morning of.

- Marinate roasts and chops overnight, chicken a few hours before the party.

- Vegetables can be prepped in advance, or blanched, parboiled, or even roasted.

- Desserts are easy—many pies and tarts, custards (flan, for one), and cakes hold up well for at least a couple of days.

- Pasta and noodle dishes are year-round comfort foods—and they make good use of farmstand produce. Same for salads made with quinoa or farro.

- For summer parties, opt for a stovetop clambake or shrimp or lobster boil, with corn and potatoes as part of the mix. Panzanella, Niçoise, and other hearty salads are other seasonal options.

- Grilling opens the doors to all kinds of meals built around fish and chops and steaks, with gremolata, romesco, salsa verde, and chimichurri (among other sauces) giving them dinner-party status.

- Build-your-own tacos and traditional curries invite guests to get involved in the assembly. Set out all the components and let everyone dig in.

SWEETS
- Dessert need not be anything more elaborate than breaking up a few bars of first-rate chocolate on a platter along with dried and/or fresh fruit (whatever is in season); and roasted almonds, hazelnuts, or pistachios.

- Mixed berries and sliced stone fruits are dessert enough in the summer. A colorful variety of sliced citrus, sprinkled with pomegranate seeds, makes a bright winter finale.

- To give any of the above a creamy component (besides whipped cream, of course), drizzle ricotta or mascarpone—or fresh goat cheese or gorgonzola dolce—with honey or maple syrup.

- There are also many make-ahead options if a more traditional dessert is called for (page 76).

4. PLOT OUT THE MENU
Once you've settled on what you'll be serving, it helps to create a timeline.

- The more detailed, the better: for example, "5:30 p.m.: Preheat oven to 350°F. Take cheeses out of the refrigerator. Chop fennel and olives. Peel and segment oranges. Chill white wine."

- Account for last-minute steps, even if you think you'll remember—it's easy to forget to add the garnishes or pie toppings.

- Include how you plan to serve everything, especially for a meal with many components—extra condiments, toasted bread, and dipping sauces, for example.

- It doesn't hurt to prepare for backups, just in case the oven fails (or you burn the roast). Have the makings for a cheese board (page 47) or a substantial salad—greens and vegetables (prepped and at the ready), canned beans or fish, even some cooked grains. Eggs and mushrooms and scallions can quickly become a skillet-to-table frittata.

5. NAIL DOWN YOUR PRE-PARTY CLEANUP

Even if you don't have the weekend to thoroughly scour your home, you can still tidy in a jiffy by being intentional. And if you've been keeping up with your daily and weekly cleaning routine, you may not even have to lift a finger.

- Focus on the important areas: entryway (or mudroom), kitchen, living room and/or dining area, and guest bathroom(s).

- Clear away all clutter—even if this means putting everything in a basket or bin (for the time being) and tucking this away in an inconspicuous spot.

- Make room near the entrance for coats and shoes and other belongings (and have a plan for bulky winter coats, such as a rented clothing rack in a bedroom).

- Straighten the living room—fluff up throw pillows, clear off the coffee table, put away stacks of half-read books and magazines. Replace any burned-out lightbulbs.

- Empty the dishwasher so you have enough tableware—and space for holding all the dirty dishes during the party.

- Glassware can get dusty or grimy on open shelves—rinse it in hot water (skip the soap, which can leave lingering odors), then dry on a rack or with a lint-free cloth.

- Wipe down the bathroom sink and toilet, and clean the mirror and hardware; put out fresh soap and hand towels. Empty the wastebasket. Make sure to provide spare toilet paper rolls. Light a candle. Add flowers.

- Clear off kitchen counters of anything that's not needed for meal prep or decoration. Take out the trash and empty the bins for recyclables.

- Lastly, clean the floors—a sure way to make a room instantly more presentable. Vacuuming is faster and more efficient than sweeping for removing dust and dirt from wood floors, plus you can use it to hit any other dusty surfaces.

6. BE PRESENT DURING THE PARTY

There's an etiquette to hosting guests. The following are tips on how to be an attentive host.

- Welcome every guest yourself—which lets you thank them for any gifts.

- Provide a place for guests to put their things, and offer to take their coats right away.

- Have snacks already set up around the space—and be sure to offer guests a drink within a few minutes of their arrival.

- Don't spend all your time in the kitchen. If you are running behind with meal prep, enlist help while you make the rounds. Or bring the party to the kitchen (if it doesn't gravitate there on its own).

- Refill water and wineglasses during a meal. Keeping pitchers of water and bottles of wine at both ends of a long table means guests can serve themselves (one less thing for you to have to remember).

- Don't rush the meal—the dessert can always wait, and it will give you time to brew the coffee and put the teakettle on.

- But do clear off plates and glasses before they have a chance to pile up (and let people help if they want to). Just wait to start cleaning all those dirty dishes until after everyone has left.

SCHEDULE

Use this checklist to help manage the elements of your get-togethers so nothing gets overlooked—and you can enjoy them as much as your friends do.

ONE OR TWO MONTHS AHEAD

☐ Decide on the style (tapas for four, dinner for eight, or a potluck).

☐ Lock down the date and time—earlier for drinks only, later for a seated dinner.

☐ Make your guest list, knowing the average acceptance rate is 80 percent (lower during summer or holidays).

☐ Invite guests; include RSVP instructions.

THREE WEEKS AHEAD

☐ Figure out your menu. Factor in the season and how much time you'll have for shopping and preparing—and be realistic.

☐ Make a shopping list, organized into non-perishables to buy right away and fresh items that need to be purchased later. Order any specialty items now.

☐ Create a recipe time-line, working back from when each dish is served. Note when make-aheads can be started and how to finish them.

☐ Check recipes for any tools you may need to buy or borrow. Same for serving pieces.

TWO WEEKS AHEAD

☐ Restock (or set up) your home bar. Plan on three bottles of wine for every four people, and two to three cocktails per guest for a two-hour party.

☐ For a large cocktail party, you'll need enough glassware; take inventory of what you have and rent extras if needed.

☐ Shop for all non-perishable items.

☐ Make your playlist.

☐ Decide on centerpieces and decorations.

ONE WEEK AHEAD

☐ Clean your home (this can be your normal weekly routine).

☐ Arrange furniture, allowing extra space for added seating. Clear off the coffee table.

☐ Follow up with any-one who has not yet RSVP'd.

A FEW DAYS AHEAD

☐ Set out serving pieces; add Post-it notes with the dish that will go in each.

☐ Finish food shopping; tackle make-aheads.

☐ Prepare decorations; place candles and vases in their spots.

☐ Switch lightbulbs for softer lighting.

☐ Clear out freezer if you need lots of ice.

THE DAY BEFORE

☐ Buy ice, if needed—plan on one pound per person (more like two pounds for a summer cocktail party outdoors).

☐ Purchase (or cut) and arrange flowers.

☐ Set the table.

☐ Do more make-aheads and prep.

☐ Create a stain-fighting kit (or make sure your regular one is ready to go in case of spills).

THE DAY OF

☐ Give your home a once-over (page 233); make a plan for coats and for holding dirty dishes.

☐ Chill wine—white, rosé, and sparkling—and beer along with appropriate mixers (page 231).

☐ Check your recipe timeline—then get everything done.

☐ Greet people and enjoy!

MARTHA MUST

My secret to getting a party started on the right foot: fruity cocktails. Start with ripe fruits—whatever is in season. Add freshly squeezed citrus and excellent spirits. Freeze some of the juice to use as "ice" cubes, too.

CELEBRATE

Whether it's a baby shower or your favorite holiday of the year (Halloween, anyone?), marking a special occasion calls for multitasking mastery, what with gifts to wrap, treats to bake, and decorations to put up. Make it easy by planning—and *doing* as much as possible—ahead of time. The tips, tricks, checklists, and meal-prep timelines on these pages will let you focus on having happy birthdays, giving thanks, and sharing the joy.

SUPPLIES

Gift-giving really kicks in during the holiday season, but you'll want to stock these items year-round to help you wrap like a pro—tags, toppers, and cards included.

ESSENTIALS	EXTRAS
☐ Card stock (for tags and cards)	☐ Bone folder and clear quilting ruler (for creasing cards)
☐ Double-sided tape	☐ Hole punch (for stringing tags) or craft punches (for decorating tags and cards)
☐ Kraft gift bags and boxes	
☐ Ribbons and twine	☐ Rotary cutter (and optional self-healing cutting mat, for more precise edges on wrapping paper)
☐ Scissors	
☐ Wrapping papers (including colorful crepe and tissue paper; also see opposite)	☐ Rubber stamps and ink pads (for embellishing tags, cards, and even packaging)

STRATEGIES

Planning and preparing for a special celebration should be part of the fun. Use the guidance here to help you navigate (and appreciate) the journey from start to finish.

1. TAKE STEPS TO ENJOY ALL YOUR CELEBRATIONS

Each holiday has its own rituals that make it so memorable (especially for little ones). Here are ways to observe those and create traditions all your own.

- Make holiday to-do lists with a targeted deadline for each task (gift buying, crafting, decorating, menu planning)—see pages 244 and 247 for two examples.

- Take inventory of what you have before buying kitchen equipment or gift-wrapping supplies or even gifts. It's easy to get caught up in the excitement and forget what you already own.

- Invite friends and family over to help decorate—it's a good excuse to spend time together in a low-key way, without all the formalities (and just have some simple drinks and snacks).

- As you unpack decorations (be they skeletons or snowflakes), weed out anything you no longer need—offer them to a local school or other group that could use some cheer.

- Once you've decorated your home, take photos of everything so you can replicate it next year (or make changes).

- When choosing a menu for holiday meals, consider making it a potluck or buffet to alleviate the effort. Otherwise, front-load it with make-aheads (aim for only two hours of cooking on the day of, Thanksgiving being the exception).

2. PLAN AHEAD FOR GIFTS AND CARDS

Last-minute shopping is not ideal, especially during the crowded holiday season. Instead, take time at the beginning of each year to map out your annual gift-giving.

MAKE GIFT LISTS (AND CHECK THEM TWICE)

- Note all birthdays, anniversaries, and other special occasions in your calendar (setting phone alerts a week ahead helps)—and keep a list of these so you can have gifts wrapped and ready.

- Make a separate list for end-of-year holiday gifts. To make shopping more efficient, organize the list by recipient, connection (family, neighbor, coworker), or interest (cook, decorator, gardener) and keep it in your phone—use the notes feature—so you can quickly glance and see what's left to buy while out and about.

- It's entirely appropriate to give just one gift to couples, neighbors, and family friends—rather than buying individual ones. Choose all-age items such as lawn games or board games; waffle irons, ice-cream makers, or popcorn poppers; or a hammock or fully stocked picnic hamper.

- Last-minute invitations are practically inevitable—as are unexpected gift exchanges. Keep a few neutral gifts—coasters, journals, candles, winter accessories, or homemade jams—in reserve to prevent splurging on something in a hurry.

UPCYCLED WRAPPINGS

Kraft paper and blank newsprint are recyclable alternatives to traditional wrapping paper—and blank canvases for your own designs.

- Soft gifts can be wrapped in attractive tea towels, cloth napkins, or even fabric remnants—and you can raid your knitting and sewing baskets for yarn, rickrack, or other scraps to use as ribbons.

- Turn pieces of wrapping paper that are ripped or too small for gifts into packing material: Run them through a paper shredder, then use (in place of Styrofoam) to protect the presents you mail. It's a great way to reduce waste.

- Save last year's holiday cards to use in making gift cards, cutting or punching them into festive shapes.

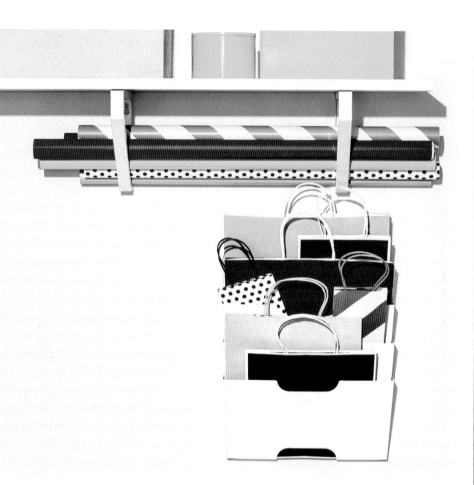

BE MINDFUL OF YOUR BUDGET

▪ Decide how much you are able to devote to gifts, and then divide that figure by the number of recipients to get a target range—and avoid impulse purchases. Factor in shipping costs and tips for service providers.

▪ Avoid adding undue stress during the holidays by putting money into a "gift fund" each month.

▪ Secret Santa exchanges save money and time on shopping. This tradition is not just for office parties—extended families often use this to ease the pressure of buying an equal gift for everyone.

▪ In lieu of gifts, consider having participants (families or colleagues or groups of friends) designate their favorite organizations for people to contribute to.

BUY GIFTS THROUGH-OUT THE YEAR

▪ Whenever you see something that reminds you of someone, buy it—you likely won't remember it later (or it may not be there when you return). Keep track of purchases on your lists.

▪ Target your purchases around seasonal sales—Memorial Day, Labor Day, Black Friday, Cyber Monday—and category-specific discounts. For example, shop for luggage in March and bicycles in October, when retailers make room for new inventory.

▪ Consider the gift card—it can be as thoughtful as a wrapped present. Giving a gift certificate to a friend's favorite independent bookstore means she gets not only a book but the enjoyment of picking it out (and you'll be supporting the seller). Just be sure to include a handwritten note saying why you chose it.

▪ Wrap gifts as soon as you bring them home (except for any going on an airplane), first taping gift receipts to packages (and including batteries for electronics). Hold off on adding toppers and tags, which might get crushed or lost during storage, but do put a Post-it on each box so you remember what's what.

▪ Create a space-saving wrapping station to keep your supplies in check such as the one above: Install a shelf near a worktable for sorting small supplies into containers on top and wrapping-paper rolls in brackets underneath; gift bags fit in a wall-mounted tiered magazine rack. Or mount pegboard and use hooks and accessories for a similar effect.

PREPARE FOR SHIPPING GIFTS BY MAIL

■ Not all giftables are suited to shipping. Obvious ones are any perishables (have those sent directly from the vendor) or items that are so large or heavy as to be cost-prohibitive. Soft goods travel well, are lightweight, and won't set you back on shipping costs.

■ Plan to ship by regular (ground) service at least two weeks before Christmas Eve—factor in weekends, too. UPS and USPS list holiday delivery dates on their websites—mark those dates on your calendar and set up digital reminders.

■ Use only sturdy boxes with flaps for fragile items; recycled boxes are fine for soft goods. Too-large boxes are prone to getting punctured or ripped when stacked, so get the right size for each gift.

■ Wrap breakables individually in packing paper, then fill the box with shredded or balled-up paper or biodegradable packing materials—but don't overstuff lest the box come apart at the seams. Use strong packing tape when assembling boxes, reinforcing the bottom for extra security.

■ When giving jewelry, consider wrapping that in a padded travel case—it will keep chains from getting tangled and be a bonus gift. Wine bottles can be sent in insulated sleeves (still adding lots of packing materials)—have them shipped by the retailer.

3. SET A FESTIVE TABLE

What do birthday bashes, baby showers, graduation send-offs—and, of course, Easter, Passover, Ramadan, Christmas, and Hanukkah—have in common? The communal table takes center stage. Make it your own.

HIGHLIGHT YOUR STYLE

If your home conveys a casual vibe, there's no need to get fancy when creating your tablescape. It's perfectly okay, for instance, to use everyday earthenware and skip the tablecloth. Even placemats are not de rigueur—just be sure to add soft touches such as cloth napkins and a table runner.

CONSIDER THE AUDIENCE

Who will be seated around the table matters—a lot. If it's a big multigenerational group, and you know certain people will expect your very finest, then you may want to pull out all the stops by using your china and crystal. Otherwise—as in a party for thirtysomethings or a bunch of close family friends—you can likely skip the formalities.

PICK A PALETTE

Modern dinnerware easily mixes with classic pieces when they're in neutral colors such as white or putty. They're also a good backdrop for bright splashes of color. You can mix and match patterned plates or napkins, too—but keeping them in the same shade helps prevent it from looking jumbled. Napkins don't even have to match—just use related colors (and/or fabrics).

THINK LOGISTICALLY

Big, bulky centerpieces take up too much space on the table and impede conversation. Arrang-

ing smaller vases and/or candles around the table keeps things simple and flexible. You can also forage for materials in your own backyard. Sculptural twigs and branches provide a surprising alternative to flowers and convey a natural beauty.

PERSONALIZE THE PLACE CARDS

Putting your own spin on the individual settings makes such a big impact—it's what people will notice first. Tailor it to the season or the occasion—working in natural elements or even your own collected trinkets.

DON'T OVERLOOK THE KIDS' TABLE

Keeping little hands occupied will buy precious time until the food arrives. Get kids to gather backyard leaves or smooth stones to make their own (or everyone's) place cards, writing their names with a silver or gold paint pen. Or line their table with coloring placemats (page 78).

MARTHA MUST

I send many gifts by mail and have discovered a way to keep bows from getting crushed in transit: Cut a tall-enough strip from a cardboard box, tape it into a round that's larger than the bow, and place it around the bow before cushioning and sealing up the box.

4. STREAMLINE YOUR HOLIDAY BAKING

Cookies and holidays go hand in hand—the more, the merrier. It's entirely possible to box up dozens (and check off your gift list) if you do a little planning and choose doughs that can be frozen (the ones here will keep up to three months).

USE MAKE-AHEAD DOUGHS

■ Icebox doughs, formed into logs for freezing, are especially convenient—just slice and bake what you need as you go. Before baking, roll the logs in sanding sugar, crushed peppermints, chopped toasted nuts, or other ingredients.

■ For making cutouts, gingerbread, sugar-cookie, and other doughs can be patted into disks, wrapped in plastic, and frozen in resealable bags. Thaw in the refrigerator before rolling out.

■ To save even more time later on, roll above doughs out to desired thickness, then freeze on a baking sheet, between layers of parchment (wrap the whole thing well in plastic). Let thaw for about ten minutes before cutting into shapes.

■ Even better, cut the rolled-out doughs into desired shapes; freeze them on parchment-lined sheets (each wrapped in plastic) and bake straight from the freezer for the same amount of time.

■ Form shortbread dough into a flat disk or square—whatever shape you plan to score it in before baking; freeze plastic-wrapped dough in a resealable plastic bag. Let thaw overnight in the refrigerator before scoring and baking.

■ You could also freeze individual drop cookies, such as oatmeal, peanut butter, or chocolate chip, on a baking sheet, and then transfer them to freezer bags. Bake still-frozen cookies on lined sheets for a few minutes longer than usual.

MAKE MULTIPLES

■ For an easy way to get more variety, prepare a big batch of sugar cookie or shortbread dough, then portion it into thirds or more and add mix-ins to each one: chopped nuts or slivered almonds; toasted spices (such as crushed fennel seeds or cardamom); crystallized ginger, citrus zest, dried fruit (currants or cranberries), or dark chocolate.

■ A cookie press makes fast work of making different shapes. The assortment of spritz cookies shown opposite all comes from a basic dough recipe. You can leave it plain; tint a portion green or another hue; add ground spices (ginger, cinnamon, allspice, and black pepper) with the dry ingredients for a spice cookie; or mix up a chocolate version by replacing part of the flour with unsweetened cocoa powder.

■ Glazes (plain or flavored with citrus juice and zest), nonpareils and sprinkles, and other toppings lend further distinction to pressed cookies, as shown, as well as simple icebox-cookie slices, shortbread, and cookie cutouts.

DECORATE WITH EASE

■ Work in assembly-line fashion. Setting up stations—rolling and cutting out shapes here, piping on details there—will help keep the (potentially messy) activity under control.

■ Schedule a bake-off and invite friends to pitch in, with cutters or presses, pastry bags and tips, white and tinted icing, and colorful sprinkles and sugars. This is especially fun for a kid's party.

■ Or host a cookie swap (see right).

COOKIE SWAP

Rather than baking multiple varieties yourself, gather friends and colleagues together for an old-fashioned cookie exchange.

■ Invite a group of six to eight—any more and guests will have to make an unwieldy number of cookies.

■ Have each person make enough of one kind of cookie to share—a dozen for sampling and another dozen for each guest to take home—and bring printouts or recipe cards for sharing (or create an online doc for everyone to copy their recipes to).

■ Set up a packaging station with kraft boxes or festive jars, tags or sticky labels, and ribbons, twine, and other trimmings.

■ At the party, sample the treats, then trade and package them in appealing assortments. Everyone leaves with finished gifts—and plenty of new recipes.

THANKSGIVING SCHEDULE

Thanksgiving is the time to break out all the shopping lists and checklists to stay on top of each and every detail of the celebration.

ONE MONTH BEFORE

- [ ] Start planning your Thanksgiving menu (see opposite).
- [ ] Order your turkey.
- [ ] Make and freeze pie doughs.
- [ ] Invite any friends or distant relatives.
- [ ] Clear out your freezer.
- [ ] Stock the bar and order wine.

THREE WEEKS BEFORE

- [ ] Confirm guest list and any food allergies or dietary restrictions.
- [ ] Organize your menu by what requires the oven, what needs stove time, and what can be made ahead.
- [ ] Check if you have enough chairs (and table space).
- [ ] Plan the kids' table (page 241).

TWO WEEKS BEFORE

- [ ] Make a shopping list and check your pantry to see what ingredients you have on hand.
- [ ] Shop for all non-perishables, cleaning supplies, and paper goods.
- [ ] Inspect your cookware, plates, and platters and buy, borrow, or rent what you need. Make sure your meat thermometer is working.
- [ ] Clean table linens.
- [ ] Plan for leftovers, stock up on supplies to send food home with your guests, and make sure you have enough storage containers for the refrigerator and freezer.

ONE WEEK BEFORE

- [ ] Clean out your refrigerator to make space.
- [ ] Buy root vegetables like sweet potatoes, and other produce that lasts, such as cranberries and apples.

THE WEEKEND BEFORE

- [ ] Write out your hour by hour cooking schedule.
- [ ] Clean sheets and linens and prep the guest room.
- [ ] Clean the house (doing your regular weekly routine).
- [ ] Make Thanksgiving crafts with the kids.

TWO TO THREE DAYS BEFORE

- [ ] Plan your Thanksgiving tablescape; DIY any decorations.
- [ ] Pick up turkey (or defrost a frozen one); buy rest of produce.
- [ ] Wash and store produce; make the cranberry sauce.
- [ ] Toast bread for stuffing and pecans for pie.

- [ ] Set the table, putting a Post-it note on each serving piece to identify the dish it will hold.

ONE DAY BEFORE

- [ ] Make your centerpiece and any place cards (now that you have your final head count).
- [ ] Defrost anything you've made ahead.
- [ ] Bake pies.
- [ ] Make dips, relishes, and salad dressing; prep as many vegetables as you can in advance.
- [ ] Pick up flowers.
- [ ] Chill wine and beer.

THANKSGIVING DAY

- [ ] Follow your hourly cooking schedule.
- [ ] Allow time for the turkey to rest before carving.
- [ ] Give thanks and savor the feast!

THE DAY AFTER

- [ ] Eat or freeze your leftovers.

MARTHA MUST

Serving buffet-style at a big gathering is most practical. I bundle the flatware by placing a fork, knife, and spoon in individual napkins. That way each guest can pick up a bundle and take it with them to their chair.

TIME-SAVING TIPS FOR THE THANKSGIVING MENU

Plan the menu

- Don't make more than you need: For a large party (10 to 12 people), figure 1½ pounds of turkey per person; smaller birds have a lower meat-to-bone ratio, so plan for 2 pounds per person in that case (and consider just cooking a turkey breast).

- If you don't have room in the refrigerator to wet-brine the bird, give it a dry rub instead: In a spice grinder, grind toasted coriander and cumin seeds with paprika, cayenne pepper, coarse salt, and black peppercorns into a powder. Rub this over the bird (pat it dry first); refrigerate at least two hours and up to 24.

- Front-load the meal with make-ahead dishes (see right) and no-cook options such as slaws and shaved-vegetable salads and a fresh cranberry relish.

- Choose sides that can be popped into the still-hot oven after the turkey comes out—roasted brussels sprouts with chestnuts, sweet potatoes with pear, green beans with hazelnuts and mushrooms, kale with garlic and golden raisins are all delicious takes on holiday favorites.

- Consider easier alternatives to traditional pie doughs—frozen puff pastry and press-in-the-pan crusts are two such options.

- If you are having a large group over, a buffet is practical and impressive.

Make these ahead

1. Many pies—with the exception of custard-style varieties (so no pumpkin pies)—can be assembled and frozen up to one month in advance, then go straight from the freezer into the oven—a worthwhile time-saver.

2. Cranberry sauces and other relishes and chutneys are often better when given a chance to meld a day or two in the refrigerator (well covered).

3. Stuffings (cooked outside the bird) and gratins can generally be assembled a day before baking and refrigerated, wrapped well in plastic. If using potatoes, submerge them completely in the liquid, such as cream or stock, to avoid oxidation (and the resulting gray color).

4. Even mashed potatoes (regular or sweet) can be kept warm for a few hours before serving: Set the covered bowl of mashed potatoes over a pot of gently simmering water, on the back of the stove top.

CHRISTMAS SCHEDULE

In the countdown to Christmas, there's no such thing as starting too early—do as much of the shopping, wrapping, cookie making, and crafting as you can before the season begins.

JANUARY (YES, REALLY!)

☐ Your holiday planning starts when storing the holiday decorations (page 17)—it's the best time to figure out what may need replacing and what you may wish to buy. Plus, you can take advantage of post-holiday discounts.

☐ Stock up on wrapping supplies (page 239), now also on sale.

☐ Prepare an end-of-year holiday gift list so you can buy gifts throughout the year.

JULY TO SEPTEMBER

☐ Make jams and pickles to give as gifts.

☐ While the weather is nice (or you're on summer vacation), snap a photo for your cards. Then place the order—or design them yourself.

☐ Plan any major home refurbishments now, when there's still time to get them done.

OCTOBER TO NOVEMBER

☐ Begin making and freezing cookie doughs.

☐ Update your gift and card list: Retire old contacts and add new ones.

☐ Prepare your home for houseguests. Make space in your entryway for their bulky coats and snow boots and winter accessories. See page 84 for more ideas.

☐ Plan a Secret Santa or other gift swap to limit purchases.

☐ Spend a few hours shopping on weekdays or after work, when stores are calmer than they are on weekends.

☐ Once Thanksgiving is over, clean oven; clear out refrigerator and freezer.

FIRST WEEK OF DECEMBER

☐ Put up an advent calendar for kids; have them write letters to Santa with their wish list.

☐ Pick out (or shop for) your holiday-party outfits and get everything ready for wearing.

☐ Send holiday cards.

☐ Plan holiday menus; order a tenderloin, ham, or other specialty foods. Choose dishes that can be made in advance and that allow you to mingle with guests rather than be tied to the kitchen.

☐ Take an inventory of baking staples, and replace those that are running low.

☐ Order a case of wine with convenient home delivery so you're ready for Christmas and New Year's celebrations.

☐ Unpack decorations, and inspect them for damaged ornaments and burned-out bulbs. Clear out any boxes with items you haven't used in a while; donate these.

☐ Pick out the holiday tree from a tree farm, nursery, or city corner. Decorate it (page 248); you'll have time to enjoy it, and it will stay fresh. Invite friends over for a tree-trimming party, with festive punch and snacks.

☐ Put up outdoor lighting and exterior decorations; greenery lasts longer outdoors.

☐ Ship gifts early to guarantee on-time delivery; save a trip to the post office by scheduling an at-home pickup at usps.com.

☐ Confirm the dates of any school concerts and celebrations.

☐ Set aside an afternoon to make cookies for teachers and class parties (if allowed).

SECOND WEEK OF DECEMBER

☐ Shop for remaining gifts—don't forget stocking stuffers!

☐ Hand out holiday tips to service providers.

KIDS

In an organized family, everyone
takes part. If that doesn't happen at your
house now, it likely won't change
overnight, but you can begin to develop
a routine that works. Start by setting up a
family calendar: It's the glue that holds
the household together, keeping
all activities, to-dos, and happenings
in one place. Then employ the
strategies that follow to help your
kids learn the organizational skills that
will serve them for life.

STRATE

**You cannot for
following steps**

1. CREATE
FAMILY
CALENDAF

Online calendar
solve your sche
snafus. Plus, the
to sync and upd
time, so nothing
dated. But you c
have success w
and pen. Here a
work it with bot
(or a combinatic

SUPP

With school
is a high pri

☐ H
C
a

☐ I
I
I
I

☐ I
I
a

☐

☐

activities. Keep track of pending registration dates for after-school classes or holiday camps along with any required paperwork or fees. Finally, note when any kids will not be home for dinner and parents' night out (in case a sitter is needed).

DOCUMENT THE DETAILS

Where appropriate, include helpful data such as location and contact information—this can be easily linked for online calendars, or you could include a sleeve for print-outs on a wall calendar or in a notebook. Whatever your method, make the family calendar a one-stop resource for everything you need to know in case there's a cancellation or just to remind yourself of who needs to be picked up when and where.

SHARE IT WITH OTHERS

Grandparents, sitters, carpooling cohorts—anyone who needs to know the schedule should ideally have access to online calendars, or take a photo of a paper one at the beginning of each week and send it to them via text or email. The beauty of online assistants is that if anything changes, all shared contacts will be notified right away—

helpful if you are in a meeting or en route and not checking messages.

BACK IT UP

If you choose the online-and-offline route, be sure to check it each morning to make sure nothing has slipped from one or the other (another reason to go all-in with digital). Either way, keep a binder of documents you rely on repeatedly—immunization records, school calendars and teacher notifications, sports rosters and schedules—in your home office or near the family command center (or scan and store these on your desktop).

2. HELP KIDS WITH TIME MANAGEMENT

In addition to the tips on page 253, these tools will help you instill in your kids the importance of being prepared.

USE A PLANNER

Kids need a way to keep track of chores, school-work, and extracurricular activities.

- That's where a weekly agenda can help; let your kids choose the one they like (and then will be more inclined to use).

- Schedule a weekly update on Sunday, populating the dates with all their events and due dates. Also, introduce kids to the idea of check-lists—it's so rewarding to tick off the "done" boxes.

CREATE DAILY ROUTINES

This way they'll know what to do even when you're not around to remind them.

- In the morning, this could be: Make the bed, shower, get dressed, eat breakfast, brush teeth, put lunchbox in backpack, and double-check school supplies.

- Account for days they come straight home from school versus those where they arrive home later, after an after-school club or other activity.

- Either way, make sure to have a regular homework routine (page 256).

- Include practice time for extracurricular activities, such as shooting hoops or playing an instrument (outside of the activities themselves).

- Also include when to do chores, such as taking out the trash or emptying the dishwasher, before or after dinner.

PROMOTE NIGHT-BEFORE PREP

Remember to model this important organizing principle as an example.

- Always make sure homework is put in the right folder and all school supplies are tucked in the backpack.

- Have any gear ready for after-school activities.

- Pick out the next day's clothes, socks, and shoes—including all accessories.

3. HONE GOOD STUDY HABITS

It's never too early to teach children the tools and techniques for self-discipline. Even toddlers can pick up good habits with a little patience and persistence.

CREATE A STUDY ZONE

The goal is to set up your child for success, both while in school and for a lifetime.

- Carve out space and furnish the desk area with shelves or open storage units to house homework supplies—and have your child help you sort and label everything to avoid the "where's my paper?" conundrum.

- Teach your kid to always study in this space (rather than sprawled out on the

SCHEDULE

Simply having a time-stamped checklist will make it easier to tick off all the boxes. Sticking to it is also key to keeping a busy household running smoothly.

DAILY

- ☐ In the morning, have old-enough kids make their own beds.
- ☐ Check backpack and sort papers; do homework.
- ☐ Check off chore list.
- ☐ Each night, set out next day's clothes; put supplies in backpack.
- ☐ Clean lunch containers; pack lunch.
- ☐ Before bedtime, kids should clean up, putting away their things.

If you have 5 minutes...
- Update contact list (teachers, coaches, sitters, carpoolers).
- Help kids straighten up their spaces.

If you have 10 minutes...
- Check craft and school supplies; make a shopping list for any replenishments.

If you have 15 minutes...
- Together, purge and sort binders and artwork throughout the year.

WEEKLY

- ☐ Review planner, binders, and online school tracker to make sure classwork is kept up.
- ☐ Have a family check-in to sync calendars.
- ☐ Create menu for school lunches; do prep-ahead tasks.

MONTHLY

- ☐ Rotate artwork on display.

TWICE A YEAR

- ☐ Purge binders at end of each semester; only keep papers deemed worthy (per each kid).

ONCE A YEAR

- ☐ At the end of the school year, file schoolwork you (and kids) decide to save, and recycle the rest.
- ☐ Sort through memory box; give away or toss any unwanted items.
- ☐ Go through artwork together; decide what to keep (page 168), what to scan (and discard original), and what to give away.

TRAVELING WITH KIDS

With some versatile supplies at the ready, your kids can keep themselves busy (no screens required!) for hours on end.

Create a craft kit:
- Choose items that are safe (no scissors) and tidy (no drippy glue): origami and scrapbook papers, washi tape, washable markers, self-adhesive gems, and stickers.
- With the above, kids can make pictures and collages—or re-create something they've seen out the window along the way.
- A container with compartments, such as a tackle box, keeps things neat and accessible.

Prepare a vacation scrapbook:
- Give each child a binder with plastic sleeves and clear zippered pencil cases.
- Kids can chronicle their trip in the car, drawing animals they see or listing the states on license plates.
- You could also give them a map of your driving (or flying) route to embellish.
- Let them take pictures on your phone of favorite spots and of the family.

Make an activity pack:
- Playing cards and travel-edition board games make the minutes fly by.
- Books with crossword puzzles and other word games sneak in teaching moments.
- Coloring books plus crayons or colored pencils keep kids (and adults!) calm and focused, even in the face of flight delays.

PETS

It takes plenty of love and good intentions to care for dogs and cats. But there's also a lot more to consider: food, training, and recreation, plus all the creature comforts to make them feel at home. Included here are suggestions for managing your furry companions' day-to-day needs (like grooming and playtime), as well as good practices for keeping them healthy and happy as the years go by.

SUPPLIES

It's all too easy to get overwhelmed (and go over budget) with a new pet, so focus first on the must-haves and pick up anything else as the need arises.

ESSENTIALS	EXTRAS
☐ Collar or harness (for dogs who pull) and leash	☐ Biodegradable waste bags (or a pooper-scooper for the backyard)
☐ Food and water bowls (plus a mat to go underneath)	☐ Crate (with soft liner)
☐ Grooming supplies (depending on the breed)	☐ Food and treat storage
☐ ID tag (for outdoor pets)	☐ Outdoor apparel (coats and booties), depending on your region
☐ Litter box (and litter!)	
☐ Pet bed	
☐ Pet-specific shampoo (and optional conditioner)	
☐ Toys (especially climbing toys for cats)	

STRATEGIES

Treat your pet's routine—exercise, feeding, appointments—as you do any other family member's: by scheduling it on your calendar. Read on for more tips.

1. BUY THE RIGHT SUPPLIES

- Many items—collars and harnesses, food and water bowls, beds and crates—depend on the size of the dog (not so much for a cat; buy these now in that case).

- Wait to buy the above if you are adopting from a shelter rather than getting your dog from a breeder, as you will usually have no way of knowing who your new four-legged friend is going to be.

- You'll also need to buy the same food your pet was eating, to ease the transition; after he's settled in, talk with your vet about switching to another food.

2. GIVE PETS THEIR OWN SPECIAL PLACE

- Fit out a spare bathroom, the mudroom, or a cozy corner of a living room with a pet bed, water bowl, and some toys.

- Just don't put them in an out-of-the-way spot like the garage—pets derive comfort from knowing their people are around, even if not in the same space.

- At least in the beginning, you may want to section off a room (or the stairs) with a baby gate—pets feel more secure when they don't have the run of the entire house, especially when home alone.

- Many dogs like to retreat to a crate with a cushioned liner—add a favorite soft toy for extra security.

- A cat might like a window perch (put a bird feeder outside for entertainment), or a wall-mounted bed (such as the repurposed basket shown here, furnished with a soft blanket for a cushion).

3. FEED PETS A HEALTHY DIET

- Adult dogs (over 1 year of age) typically need two meals a day; puppies often require three or four. Felines (young and old) may prefer more frequent smaller meals, but avoid overfeeding (ask your vet).

- Follow the food-package recommendations—and your vet's advice—for the total daily amount; divide that by number of meals.

- Monitor your pet's weight with what is called a body-conditioning scoring test: Looking at it from above, the abdomen should be narrower than the hips and chest; from the side, the chest should be lower to the ground than the belly; and when rubbing, you should just barely be able make out the ribs. Then adjust daily food accordingly.

- Make sure pets always have access to fresh water—and replace it often (cats are especially finicky about the smell). Wash the bowl at least once a day.

- And because cats aren't so good at drinking water on their own, many vets recommend giving them wet food over dry—or at least a combination. Talk about this with your vet.

4. WALK THE DOG EVERY DAY

- For bathroom breaks, a puppy can hold its urine one more hour than its age in months; by month six, a dog should go out every six to eight hours.

- When it comes to exercise, aim for two walks a day—dogs are stimulated by all the scents outdoors. A brisk walk around the block is fine for low-energy and older dogs; otherwise, aim for a 20- to 30-minute stint at a panting pace.

- On inclement-weather days, play fetch or tug-of-war in a hallway or the basement, or hide treats around the home for a game of hide-and-seek.

- Stash leashes and waste bags by the door for easy grabbing on your way out.

5. MAKE TIME TO PLAY WITH FELINES

- It's easy to assume these independent animals can fend for themselves, but cats benefit from enrichment the same as dogs do.

- Channel a cat's natural tendencies with climbing toys, such as a tiered "cat condo," or let her play with paper bags and boxes.

- Laser pointers and battery-operated mice prompt hide-and-seek play and predatory behavior.

- "Play" can also include any activity that breeds bonding—training, grooming, even lounging together on the sofa.

- Aim for a few 15-minute stints throughout the day.

6. BATHE AND GROOM AS NEEDED

- Daily toothbrushing is recommended, though even a few times a week is better than nothing. Use a soft toothbrush (or finger cot) and pet-specific toothpaste; baking soda wipes are good for pets who won't tolerate a brush, as are dental chews.

- Most pets should be bathed every four to six weeks—more often in case of an oily coat or allergy. (Cats can probably go longer between bathings—and may need a trip to the groomer.) Don't overdo it—too-frequent bathing (and hot water) can cause dry skin and more dander.

- A nonslip mat is helpful for the tub, shower, or sink; use a gentle pH-balanced shampoo and optional conditioner for pets (never human products).

- Even short-haired breeds benefit from having their coats brushed every now and then (to keep them shiny); for long-haired dogs and cats, pick a deshedding tool that you and your pet find comfortable and use it daily.

- Guillotine-style nail trimmers are best for small to medium-size dogs, scissor clippers for large dogs. Either works for cats, but with the former you run less risk of cutting into the nail's quick. (Or have the groomer do this for you.)

- Smush-nose cats and dogs are prone to tear stains (and bacterial build-up) under their eyes; use a gentle pet-specific formula to clean this area.

7. KEEP TOYS IN CHECK

- To keep your pet stimulated, rotate out a third of his playthings every few weeks, putting the rest in a bin in a spare closet.

- Pets can get overstimulated (and then stop playing) if there are too many toys around; leave a few favorites out at a time.

- For safety, don't leave out toys with small removable parts or long strings; discard any toys with exposed batting.

8. STAY ON TOP OF HEALTH CARE

- Most adult dogs and cats should see the vet once or twice a year for routine examinations.

- Puppies and kittens will require more visits to monitor development, and seniors may benefit from being put on a pain-management protocol.

- Include an annual dental evaluation—85 percent of pets suffer from dental disease by age 3.

- Your vet will be able to advise you on the frequency of immunizations, which varies by state.

- Keep up with preventive heartworm and flea-and-tick medications year-round—and check for ticks when advisable.

- Don't save up concerns for regular visits, since early detection is key to a better prognosis (and pets are sneaky about hiding pain). Pay close attention to your pet's activity level, appetite, and attitude—any unusual and sudden changes merit a call to the vet.

LIVING WITH PETS

With pets as your housemates, take these steps to maintain a clean living space.

Keep pets clean. Use unscented wipes on pets between baths, whenever they could use a refresh. Stow wipes by the door, too, to clean off grimy paws. Put a mat outside the litter box to keep cats from tracking dirt.

Eliminate pet hair and dander. Brush pets regularly and preferably outdoors. Go over furniture and other surfaces with a lint brush each day or as needed. Launder pet bedding and soft toys weekly on the hottest cycle; add baking soda to the wash for strong odors.

Treat accidents right away. Start by blotting up liquids with a rag or old towel. Then gently clean the soiled area with a mild dishwashing liquid diluted with water, and dab with plain water and a clean towel to rinse. To remove odors and stop a pet from returning to the scene of the crime, saturate the area with an enzyme-based odor neutralizer, such as Nature's Miracle, and let dry.

SCHEDULE

Be sure to block time for important events like vet visits in the family calendar (see page 253). You'll also want to use this checklist to keep track of all the rest.

DAILY

- [ ] Feed and provide fresh water; wash food and water bowls.

- [ ] Walk the dog twice a day (weather permitting; or enrich him indoors); schedule in playtime for cats.

- [ ] Brush your pet's teeth—or provide dental chew treats/toys.

- [ ] Brush long-haired dog and cat breeds (to prevent matting).

- [ ] Scoop out waste and soiled litter from cat box.

- [ ] Go over fabrics and bedding with a lint brush.

- [ ] Check dog for ticks after a romp in the woods (or backyard) depending on your region.

- [ ] Treat accidents right away.

WEEKLY

- [ ] Empty litter box and clean thoroughly with warm soapy water and a rag or dedicated sponge; let air-dry thoroughly before refilling.

- [ ] Clean floor around pet feeding area.

TWICE MONTHLY

- [ ] Launder pet bedding and soft toys in hot water with unscented detergent; use non-chlorine bleach to remove stains or caked-in dirt.

- [ ] Do the same when washing outdoor apparel (coats and jackets) during the winter.

MONTHLY

- [ ] Stay current on flea and tick prevention and heartworm medications.

- [ ] Bathe dog or cat and clip nails (or take to the groomer).

- [ ] Give your pet a thorough once-over to look for growths or other developments.

- [ ] Rotate out toys (to keep them stimulated).

- [ ] Replenish supply of baby wipes and biodegradable waste bags in entry or mudroom.

SEASONALLY

- [ ] Bring out (or put away) cold-weather outdoor dog apparel (including booties or pet-safe paw wax).

TWICE A YEAR

- [ ] Take your pet for a routine vet examination (more frequently for puppies and kittens).

ONCE A YEAR

- [ ] Schedule a thorough dental evaluation.

- [ ] Celebrate their birthday with hugs and kisses (and homemade dog biscuits).

PET SAFETY

- Your pet should never leave home without a tag that includes your own or your vet's contact information (and always get your pet microchipped).

- If you walk your dog before or after daylight hours, use a reflective collar or harness to keep him visible in the dark.

- Stock a first-aid kit with basic items (ask your vet) that can address scrapes and other minor mishaps.

- Put an "In Case of Fire" sticker (available online or from your local fire department) on main entrances to alert first responders of any pets that need rescuing.

WELLNESS

Just as there are tools for tending
the garden or making household repairs,
there are supplies and strategies for
self-care—and they're every bit as critical.
The advice on these pages will help you
boost your health and well-being
by prioritizing exercise, good-quality
sleep, and a whole-foods approach
to eating, plus mindfulness, meditation,
and other practices. Read on
for the best ways to help yourself.

SUPPLIES

Making quality time for yourself will be easier with these feel-good items. Keep in mind that some, if not all, of these extras may be high-priority for you.

ESSENTIALS	EXTRAS
☐ Books (and other reading materials)	☐ Aromatherapy aids (diffusers and essential oils)
☐ Exercise gear (shoes, yoga mat, free weights)	☐ Bath salts and exfoliating scrubs or brushes (see page 22 for some suggestions)
☐ Journals (one for practicing gratitude, another for keeping on a nightstand)	☐ Earbuds (for listening to music or podcasts)
☐ Reuseable water bottle (for taking with you while exercising) and carafe (for hydrating at home or work)	☐ Humidifier
	☐ Protein snacks
☐ Skin care products (including sunscreen)	☐ Sleep mask
☐ Well-stocked pantry (page 215)	☐ Tea (preferably loose tea leaves steeped in a reusable tea ball or compostable sachets)

STRATEGIES

Start by blocking time in your planner for me-time—and be specific, such as "read a book at the park." If you don't make the time, you won't take the time.

1. TAKE CHARGE OF YOUR DAY IN LITTLE WAYS

Work, parenting, and other adult daily duties can be draining, but it's the niggling tasks that can zap energy and leave you tapped out. Fortunately even subtle shifts can revive you.

BREATHE EASY

Meditation is most effective in the early a.m. hours, when your mind is clear—and connecting with your inner self will set you up for the day ahead. Before you tumble out of bed, spend a quiet five to ten minutes (or more if you like) doing your method of choice; see page 274 for more tips on how to be mindful.

PACE YOURSELF

Try saving your first cup of coffee or tea until you're at work, when it can pack more of a punch—caffeine is less effective when you've been awake only an hour or two. Drinking coffee later in the morning will help lessen the impact of the afternoon slump.

RECONSIDER YOUR COMMUTE

Being stuck in traffic or a crowded subway car can seriously mess with your mood. If possible, alter your trip. Map out new routes and tactics. Build in exercise by biking or walking (even if only part of the way). If nothing else, take steps to keep your brain moving— tune into an inspiring audiobook or humorous podcast, or chat with a friend to preempt the negative thinking.

BE MORE PRESENT

Constantly scrolling through social media chips away at your ability to focus—so maybe you end up starting tasks but not finishing them. To break the cycle, take note of when you get the twitch to check your phone—then set rules around those times, like putting the phone in a drawer. Even better, but harder: Ask yourself what you're really seeking (connection with others? a good laugh?) and try to get that in real time.

POWER THROUGH

Don't succumb to the four-o'clock snack attack—plan your own protein-packed energizers. Almond butter and apple slices, full-fat yogurt and berries, prosciutto and cantaloupe. If you must resort to an energy bar, make sure it has fewer than five ingredients, less than 4 grams of sugar, and at least 3 grams of fiber.

GIVE YOUR EYES A REST

Even if you don't have 20-20 vision, you can remember this practical approach: After every 20 minutes of computer work, look up and focus on a spot 20 feet away for 20 seconds. Also, try to blink more often, and carry tear-replacement drops to combat dry-eye syndrome.

STAND UP

Sitting for hours at a time is not conducive to productivity, creativity, or good health. Stand up at least once an hour—preferably for 15 to 30 minutes at a stretch. Refill your water bottle or venture outside for fresh air.

FIRST-AID KIT

Here's a checklist of items recommended by the Red Cross (you can also order one of their kits online). Keep the kit out of reach of children, but be sure to let all caregivers know where to find it.

- Sterile gauze pads (in different sizes) and adhesive tape
- Adhesive bandages in several sizes
- Elastic bandage
- Antiseptic wipes and solution (like hydrogen peroxide)
- Antibiotic ointment
- Hydrocortisone cream (1%)
- Pain relief medication
- Tweezers
- Sharp scissors
- Disposable instant cold packs (and keep two reusable ones in the freezer)
- Calamine lotion
- Thermometer
- Non-latex gloves (two pairs)

2. SCHEDULE IN EXERCISE

The American Heart Association recommends 150 minutes of exercise per week at a moderate intensity, where you're too breathless to sing but still able to talk. That breaks down to 30 minutes five days a week—and those need not be consecutive.

■ Get outdoors, preferably with a friend, when possible. You're likely to feel more motivated, burn more calories, and gain more enjoyment when you combine nature with this form of nurture.

■ Variety is the best way to benefit the whole body. Too much of any single type of exercise can lead to overuse injuries—that's why marathoners rotate long and short runs with low-impact stints (swimming or cycling). Stop when you feel pain—it's a signal from your body.

■ For the ultimate all-body workout, try cross-training, choosing one workout from each category— cardio, strength, and flexibility—at least once a week. For example: Monday, pick one cardio activity (running, biking, using an elliptical machine, Zumba dancing); Wednesday, select a

strength-training exercise (TRX, Pilates, sculpting class, weight lifting); Friday, focus on flexibility (yoga, qigong, stretch class); Saturday, circle back to cardio.

■ It's helpful to be able to practice yoga on your own—classes are often at inconvenient times, and also in the event of snow days or while traveling.

Carve out a nook and add a candle or diffuser. Take out your earbuds and power down the phone.

■ Doing the same series of poses—and at the same time of day—will help you go with the flow. Even ten minutes a day will make a difference—bundle it with your daily meditation (page 271) for optimal results.

3. MAKE SLEEP A PRIORITY

Seven to eight hours is enough for most adults. Too little and you hazard more than just crankiness. Insufficient sleep is also associated with diabetes, hypertension, obesity, depression, and cognitive decline. Here are the ABCs of getting enough ZZZs.

- Exercising early in the day is believed to have the greatest benefit on sleep—but any physical exertion is better than nothing.

- Watch what you eat and drink. Cut off caffeine at noon (it stays in the body for 12 hours) and alcohol three hours before bed—that also goes for eating heavy, spicy foods. Load up on food rich in magnesium, a natural muscle relaxant—chickpeas, lentils, sunflower seeds, and spinach.

- Experts recommend going to bed and waking up at around the same time each day (including on weekends). When that's not possible, such as when traveling or if your work hours fluctuate, at least try to get the same number of sleep hours in. Just count backward from your ideal wake-up time to find the proper bedtime. If you hit the snooze button on the alarm clock, you're not getting enough sleep.

- Establish a nightly ritual. About an hour before your target bedtime, swap out any stimulating or stress-inducing activities (checking your work email) for something more relaxing—knitting, stargazing, reading a book. Taking a warm bath or shower before bedtime can also promote better sleep.

- Keep a notepad next to your bed to jot down anything that is occupying your mind (and keeping you awake). If you wake up and simply cannot fall back to sleep, get out of bed and read (no screens!) or meditate; deep breathing alone has been shown to be effective. Tossing and turning will only ramp up your stress level.

- A dark, quiet room is the most conducive to sound sleep. Use blackout shades in bedrooms; a sleep mask is another (easier) option. Put light dimmers on bedside lamps. Dim the light setting on your phone (and flip it over, face down); put it on do-not-disturb mode. Use sleep earplugs or create ambient noise with a phone app or a fan.

- Program the nightly thermostat to 65°F, considered the ideal temperature for sound sleep. Keep a lightweight blanket at the foot of the bed.

- Make your bedroom a sanctuary of sleep. If possible, avoid having exercise equipment or the home office here. Opt for lavender, jasmine, and other houseplants that are believed to be sleep aids. Use aromatherapy diffusers or essential oils (sprinkle some on your sleep mask or pillowcases).

4. EAT FOR YOUR HEALTH (AND SATISFACTION)

Focus on real food—and build healthy habits around it. Doing so, and implementing the following principles, will have you eating well in the moment and also for life.

- Eat a wide variety of foods to get the full range of essential nutrients, prioritizing seasonal produce and plant-based proteins.

- Picture this on your plate: Fill half with vegetables, one-quarter with whole grains, and the rest with lean protein; healthy oils and fats go in the middle (avocado, olives, or nuts and seeds).

- Cook meals for yourself, including daily breakfast and lunch and at least three or four dinners a week. Figure out simple weekday meals that you enjoy enough to eat on a regular basis. See pages 218 to 225 for ideas and inspiration. Always keep the ingredients for those meals on hand (see page 215 for shopping tips).

- Aim for 25 to 38 grams of fiber daily—easy enough to do if you make a few tweaks to what you already eat. Add lentils (which have 8 grams of fiber per ½ cup) to your regular salad, for example, and you've already met a quarter of your quota. Sub white flour with whole wheat flour for four times the fiber.

- Embrace, rather than eliminate, carbohydrates—the good kind are full of fiber and satisfying. Stock up on brown rice, barley, and other whole grains; sweet potatoes and regular potatoes (fries don't count); parsnips, beets, and other root vegetables; and black beans, lentils, and other legumes.

MARTHA MUST

I drink my first glass of water at 5 a.m., and during the day I keep a carafe of lemon water within reach so I can satisfy my thirst, letting my body dictate the quantity it needs.

MORNING ROUTINE REBOOT

These simple shortcuts will streamline your steps, unclutter your shelves, and make every minute (and product) count.

- Prep the night before to avoid the morning scramble. In the evening, set out your clothes and shoes and pack your bag for the next day. Make or at least plan for breakfast and brown-bag lunches.

- Multitask in the shower. When shampooing, treat yourself to a scalp massage. While your conditioner does its job, lather up your body (and do any shaving) and detangle your hair. End with a blast of cold water to tone your face (hot water can dry out skin) and give shine to hair.

- Buff as you dry. One of the simplest exfoliants is your towel. Use it to remove dead skin cells and allow young ones to reach the surface. Start at your feet and work in an upward direction to keep skin taut.

- Cut drying time and protect your tresses. Blow-drying sopping-wet hair causes more damage than good, and takes much longer. Instead, wrap your hair in a towel and go about your beauty routine. This way you can also blow hair dry in a steam-free bathroom (less frizz), or let air-dry.

- Combine makeup and sunscreen in a single step. For fail-safe coverage, mix a few drops of your regular foundation into a dollop of tinted sunscreen (at least SPF 15).

- Brush lips along with teeth. Use the toothbrush's bristles to gently scrub your lips, making your lips soft and supple, and your lipstick apply more evenly.

- Make sure to get enough protein—it's essential to healthy muscles (including your heart) and provides the fuel to keep you going all day. If you are forgoing meat and chicken, opt for fish (preferably wild-caught salmon, sardines, and mackerel), eggs, and plant-based proteins such as beans and legumes.

- Skip dairy if you must (and consider taking a calcium supplement). Otherwise, enjoy it at its richest and creamiest—the fat can be a source of valuable nutrients. Whole-milk products, whether cheese or yogurt, will also be the least processed.

- Banning all sweets can backfire; instead, enjoy them only occasionally (and watch out for sugary energy bars and fruit-flavored yogurt). By savoring sugary treats less often, you'll lose your craving for them—and find satisfaction from fresh fruit or a square of dark chocolate.

- Slow down, turn off all screens, and pay attention to the food before you. You'll feel sated before overdoing it (what the Japanese call *hara hachi bu*) and derive more emotional fulfillment (and greater mindfulness).

5. PRACTICE MINDFULNESS

Being present yields better focus, greater clarity, and improved mental and emotional well-being. When you are struggling to be productive or stuck in a negative-thought loop, look to the following tips for a healthful solution.

BREATHE DEEPLY

Even 25 minutes a day of meditation, with breath as a key component, can reduce stress.

- Block out periods of time—5 to 15 minutes, morning and afternoon—on your calendar; or at least build in a few minutes here and there throughout the day.

- You can meditate just as effectively sitting at a desk or lying in the grass. Put your phone on airplane mode (and keep it out of eyesight) until you're done.

- Allow your breath to naturally get deeper and slower and smoother—don't try to force it. This alone will help take your mind to a quieter place.

- When your mind begins to wander (it happens), refocus on your breathing.

Think of it as developing a discipline of concentration, which will help you be in the moment and experience greater awareness.

■ To ease you into the practice, download an app with guided meditations or sign up for a local class.

PRACTICE GRATITUDE

The more grateful you are (studies show), the better for your mental health, relationships, quality of work, and creativity.

■ Keep a gratitude journal and establish a gratitude ritual—upon waking or before heading off to sleep, for example, and blocking this time on your schedule. Note three things you are thankful for each day.

■ In addition, take time to write down expressions of gratitude during negative moments to combat anger and anxiety and trigger positive emotions.

■ Even a one-time act of gratitude (sending a thank-you note, treating a friend to tea) can cause a spike in happiness—and with it, greater productivity.

■ Helping others (and receiving gratitude) promotes a similar result, creating a give-and-get loop that benefits everyone.

GARNER ACCEPTANCE

Being mindful means accepting each moment as it comes—and yourself as you are.

■ Self-criticism drains energy; focus on your successes—even small ones.

■ Resist the tendency to measure your happiness by that of others—a side effect of social media.

■ Define your own sense of fulfillment, then pursue things that reinforce that.

■ Remind yourself that fear of failure and rejection is just part of human nature. Don't let these negative feelings stop you from striving for goals.

■ Just be sure to have realistic goals—don't set yourself up for failure. Reward yourself for accomplishments (with all due humility).

■ Acceptance does not mean denial or avoidance; it's important to always acknowledge your mistakes and use them as a catalyst for positive change and self-improvement.

SCHEDULE: PREVENTIVE HEALTH

Health-care needs change over time. The chart below helps you know the risks and concerns at each stage of life so you can be proactive in always feeling your best.

AGE	OVERVIEW	THE BIGGEST RISKS
In Your 20s	This is prime time to set yourself up for decades to come—eat a healthy diet, get enough exercise, and be serious about sun prevention by applying SPF moisturizer every day.	The skin cancer melanoma is among the more prevalent cancers that can strike young women. Make regular visits to the dermatologist to chart any changes. Also see your gynecologist for present wellness and to avoid infertility issues sometimes caused by STDs.
In Your 30s	Issues affecting menstruation and pregnancy are significant now. If you want to have a child, it may be harder to become pregnant as your fertility wanes after about age 35. General self-care is also a top priority.	Cancer is the most common cause of death for women starting at age 35. Talk to your doctor about any specific risk factors and family history that might merit screening tests for particular types.
In Your 40s	A decade before you have your last period, your menstrual cycle may begin to change, from longer to shorter, lighter to heavier, or vice versa. This is the perimenopausal decade.	The risk of cancer more than doubles at age 45 (through 54); inform your doctor of any family history. The risk of diabetes also goes up at age 45, and can lead to heart and kidney disease among other serious problems. Fortunately, lifestyle changes can help with the prognosis.
In Your 50s	Menopause brings about many changes, from bone loss and hot flashes to mood swings and depression. All are normal—and can interfere with sleep, so it's crucial to build in relaxation (page 271).	Although cancer is still at the top of the list of health risks during your 50s, heart disease is not far behind, and increases substantially for 55-plus women.
In Your 60s	Stay limber in body and mind, the best way to keep physical and mental decline at bay. Continued good nutrition (with plenty of protein) and regular exercise are essential.	Beware of diseases of the bone (osteoporosis) and the eye (cataracts, glaucoma, and macular degeneration) during this time. Monitor your blood pressure and cholesterol levels, as heart disease poses the most risk for women over 65.
In Your 70s	Falls can lead to fractures, so take precautions. Do strength-training for muscle tone, balance, and bone health, and learn something new to exercise your mind.	Heart disease and cancers are the leading causes of death in women now, as are stroke and chronic lower-respiratory disease. Joint issues, as a result of arthritis, may become troublesome.

KEY TESTS/VACCINES	SUPPLEMENTS
Get a Pap test every three years and cholesterol testing every four to six years. Women with a family history of cancer should discuss being screened for breast-cancer susceptibility genes BRCA1 or BRCA2 after the age of 18.	It's never too early to support bone health; get the RDAs of calcium and vitamin D. A B-complex vitamin can help with PMS and also boost energy; vitamin C helps with iron absorption.
Help stave off the flu with an annual flu shot. Even pregnant or breastfeeding women should get the vaccine. If you don't see a dermatologist for annual skin-cancer screenings, start now. Continue with Pap and HPV testing every five years.	If you plan to have children, start taking at least 400 mg of folic acid daily, and at least a month before pregnancy; iron is also recommended if your blood levels are low (ask your doctor).
Age 40 is when a comprehensive eye exam is recommended and when many women get their first mammogram (age 45 if you have no risk factors). Monitor your blood sugar and blood pressure levels.	To keep bones strong as you head toward menopause, get 1,000 mg of calcium and 600 IUs of vitamin D daily; omega-3 fatty acids help regulate mood swings and fight inflammation.
Schedule your first colonoscopy (if you haven't had one sooner). Have annual cholesterol checks, and get a baseline bone-density test two years after your last period (sooner if you have risk factors).	Continue taking omega-3s as well as calcium in conjunction with vitamin D; a B complex vitamin helps with energy, sleep, mood swings, and cardiovascular health, as does magnesium.
Get regular colonoscopies (depending on your risk factors) and annual eye exams. After 55, mammograms drop to every two years. The shingles vaccine is recommended at age 60, the pneumonia vaccine at 65. If you haven't yet, get a bone-density exam.	Keep up with omega-3s and vitamin D. Vitamins A and C are potent anti-agers; vitamin A also helps support eye health, as does lutein.
Continue many of the same ones you had in your 60s: bone-density and cholesterol tests, eye exams, and mammograms (colonoscopies can stop at 76). Get hearing tests—and the high-dose flu shot—every year.	Vitamin B12 is essential for brain functioning; (even a mild deficiency can lead to dementia); vitamin D boosts overall immunity. Protein powder or pills help rebuild muscle loss.

TEMPLATES

HEART-SHAPED CAKE

See "Bake Heart-Shaped Sweets," page 23.

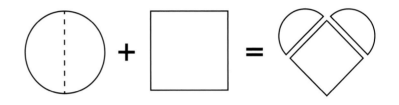

RUFFLED-HEART VALENTINE

See "Make Valentine's Day Cards," page 22. Photocopy template at desired size.

DAISY-CHAIN PUMPKIN

See "Carve Pumpkins," page 73. Photocopy template at desired size.

INDEX

A

accessories, 94, 118, 138, 140–41
annual tasks. *See* yearly tasks
appliances
　cleaning, 184, 185
　heating and cooling, 207
　kitchen, 79, 101, 102, 108, 209
　laundry, 145, 146, 180, 191, 207
　life spans, 207
April, 32–37
artwork
　decorating with, 93, 124, 128, 135
　hanging, 209
　kids', 49, 168
August, 56–61

B

backyards. *See* yards
baking. *See also* cooking
　cakes, 23
　cookies, 23, 34, 84, 242
　for gifts, 83, 242
　for holidays, 23, 34, 52, 76, 83, 84, 242, 245, 249

with maple syrup, 29
　pies, 52, 67, 76, 245
baskets and bins
　for bathrooms, 115, 116
　for bedrooms, 135, 136
　for closets, 84, 94, 138, 141
　for craft supplies, 152, 168
　for decorations, 17
　for entertaining, 46, 233
　for entryways, 84, 89, 92, 93
　general usage, 11
　for guests, 84
　for kids' rooms, 165, 166, 168, 170
　for kitchens, 98, 101, 102, 107, 108, 116
　for laundry rooms, 146, 148, 149, 190
　for living rooms, 127
　for offices, 152, 154, 159
　for pets, 263, 265
　for utility spaces, 173, 174, 175, 209
bathrooms, 114–21
　cleaning, 184, 185
　cosmetics, 120–21
　designing for relaxation, 116
　evaluating, 116
　storage, 118

bedding. *See also* blankets
　laundering, 41, 145, 189, 190, 191
　for pets, 52, 263, 267
　seasonal, 41, 65
　storage, 25, 133, 135, 175
　tips, 136
bedrooms, 132–41. *See also* kids' rooms
　accessories, 140–41
　beds and nightstands, 136
　closets, 138
　evaluating, 135
　storage, 135, 138–41
　tidying, 135
bee houses, 54
bicycles, 31
bins. *See* baskets and bins
blankets. *See also* bedding
　for the car, 47, 53, 77
　for guests, 84
　laundering, 189
　for pets, 263
　picnic, 53
　seasonal, 65
　storage, 127, 135, 136
bookcases
　cleaning, 24
　for kids' rooms, 166
　organizing, 128
　as room dividers, 124

books
　cookbooks, 35, 102, 225
　displaying, 127, 128, 154
　kids', 165, 166
boxes. *See also* baskets and bins
budgeting
　for furniture, 127
　for gifts, 240
　for groceries, 218
　for home maintenance, 207
buffets, 239, 244, 245
bulletin boards, 90, 151, 166

C

cabinets
　bathroom, 116, 118
　kitchen, 97, 98, 101, 104
　laundry room, 146
　for media devices, 128, 130
　office, 152
　utility, 174
cakes, 23
calendars. *See also* monthly calendars
　family, 253–54
　mounted, 173
cards. *See also* gifts
　for holidays, 22, 40, 85
　reusing, 239

cars
  summer kits, 47
  warming, 25
  winterizing, 72, 77
carts
  bar, 130
  for kitchens, 101
  laundry, 146
  for offices, 152
casseroles, 221
ceiling racks, 98, 102, 174
celebrations, 236–49. *See also* entertaining; holidays
  gifts for, 239–41
  schedules, 244–49
  strategies for, 239–42
  supplies for, 238
  table settings for, 241
chairs. *See* seating
chalkboards, 93, 166
chests, 127, 135, 136
Christmas
  cookies, 84, 242
  decorations, 17, 82
  gifts, 83, 240–41
  schedules, 247–48
  trees, 17, 82, 247, 248
cleaning, 178–85. *See also* laundry; stains
  beach towels, 61
  ceiling fans, 46
  dusting, 65, 182
  before entertaining, 233
  grills, 29
  ovens, 79
  patios and porches, 185
  pets, 93, 265, 267
  rugs, 30
  schedules, 184–85
  shoes and boots, 35, 93
  siding, 29

  silverware, 77
  sponges, 101
  strategies for, 181–82
  swimwear, 49
  technology, 160
  tips, 184–85, 191
  windows, 34
  wood floors, 182
cleaning supplies, 180
  DIY cleansers, 182
  storage, 101, 116, 175, 184
clips, 168, 190
closets
  bedroom, 137
  entryway/hall, 94
  kids', 165
  laundry, 146
  linen, 25
clothing. *See also* laundry
  folding, 138
  hanging, 94, 138, 190
  kids', 165
  mending, 149, 189
  protecting, 138, 140
  seasonal, 65, 141
  storage, 92–94, 135, 138, 175
cocktails, 40, 53, 235
collectibles, 98, 128, 166
color-coding, 94, 165, 253
comforters, 136
composting, 37, 70, 110, 195, 198
containers
  for bathrooms, 118
  for cleaning supplies, 101
  for craft supplies, 168, 171
  decorative, 93, 138, 157

  for folded items, 175
  for food storage, 11, 79, 106, 110, 111
  for laundry supplies, 148, 149
  for office supplies, 154, 156
cookies, 23, 34, 84, 242
cooking, 212–25. *See also* baking; In-Season Picks; pantries; recipes and tips
  big-batch, 221
  casseroles, 221
  for gifts, 25, 83
  grocery shopping, 218
  make-aheads, 231, 242, 245, 249, 257
  no-cook meals, 55
  planning for, 65, 218, 232–33, 257
  prepping, 102, 106
  presentations, 47
  preserving, 222–23
  roasting, 220, 221
  schedules, 225
  strategies for, 215–23
  supplies, 214
  on vacation, 59
cords and chargers, 93, 124, 136, 152
cosmetics, 116, 118, 120, 121
couches. *See* seating
craft projects
  coloring placemats, 78
  coloring wall, 171
  folded heart notes, 22
  leaf art, 73
  map coasters, 48
  painted wooden eggs, 35
  paper ghosts, 72
  paper snowflakes, 85

  thumbprint animals, 40
crafts
  displaying, 49, 168
  supplies and storage, 168, 170–71, 256
  while traveling, 259
  workspaces, 152, 165
cubbies, 93, 94, 128, 131, 136, 166

D

daily tasks
  cleaning, 181, 184
  cooking, 225
  kids, 254, 256, 259
  laundry, 191
  lawn and garden, 202
  office, 159, 160
  pets, 264, 267
December, 80–85
decks, 31, 185, 207
decorating. *See also* artwork; flowers; houseplants
  bathrooms, 116
  bedrooms, 133, 135, 136
  closets, 138
  displays, 60
  entryways, 93
  focal points, 124
  for holidays, 17, 35, 72, 73, 82, 85, 247, 248
  with keepsakes, 60
  kids' rooms, 49, 163, 165, 168
  kitchens, 98, 102
  living rooms, 124, 127, 128, 130, 131
  offices, 154

DIY
    accessories organizer, 140
    bungee-cord shelves, 154
    cleansers, 182
    coloring wall, 171
    command center, 90
    credenza, 130
    cubby station, 166
    ironing board, 146
    miniature "forests," 198
    ottoman, 131
    pesticides, 197
    supplies pocket, 156
    tool kits, 209
    under-shelf storage, 171
    wall hangers, 89
documents. See papers
donating. See purging
drawers
    for accessories, 140
    for craft supplies, 170
    dividers and inserts, 11, 104, 106–7, 157
    for kitchen tools, 98, 106–7
    for office supplies, 157
duvets, 136, 145

E

Earth Day, 37
Easter, 34, 35
eco-friendly tips. See also composting; Earth Day
    bags, 218
    cars, 25
    cleaning, 79, 182, 184–85
    conserving energy, 208

food packaging, 79, 83, 107, 257
    pesticides, 197
entertaining, 226–35. See also celebrations
    food and drinks, 47, 130, 229–33
    hosting, 233
    schedules, 235
    seating for, 124
    stains, 85
    stations, 46, 130
    strategies for, 229–33
    supplies for, 228
entryways, 88–95
    closets, 94
    command centers, 90
    evaluating, 90
    personalizing, 93
    storage, 92–94
exercise. See wellness

F

family
    calendars, 253–54, 256–57
    command centers, 254
    meetings, 253
fans, ceiling, 46, 55, 209
Father's Day, 48
February, 20–25
filing. See also papers
    digital, 160
    storage, 154
    systems, 159
financial planning, 16
first-aid kits, 271
flea market finds, 102, 163, 175
floor plans, 124, 127

flowers. See also gardening
    arrangements, 41, 199
    gardening, 28, 195
    lilacs, 41
    orchids, 30
    planting bulbs, 64
food safety, 49, 78, 112–13
food storage
    containers, 11, 106, 111
    for dry goods, 110, 112
    for perishables, 108, 113
Fourth of July, 52
foyers. See entryways
fruits. See produce
furniture
    bathroom, 115, 116
    bedroom, 135–36
    for crafting, 168, 170
    entryway, 89, 93
    kids', 163, 165
    kitchen, 98, 102
    living room, 124, 127, 131
    multi-tasking, 11, 127, 131, 135
    office, 152
    rearranging, 43
    repair kits, 209
furoshiki, 25

G

garages. See utility spaces
gardening, 192–203. See also houseplants
    bed marking, 35, 197
    bulbs, 64
    care while away, 55, 199–201
    cleanup, 28
    container gardening, 43
    fertilizing, 28, 55, 201

mulch, 17, 70
pest control, 49, 197
planning, 195, 197
planting and nurturing, 198–99
potting benches, 201
pruning, 24, 199
schedules, 202–3
seasonal, 28, 36, 61, 64
shopping for, 65, 196
strategies for, 195–201
supplies for, 194
tools, sharpening, 25
trees, container-grown, 36
vegetables and herbs, 54, 55, 70, 202
weeding, 199
gifts. See also cards
    with batteries, 85
    for Christmas, 83
    for Father's Day, 48
    from the kitchen, 25, 83, 242
    lists, 239
    for the new year, 17
    purchasing, 240
    shipping, 241
    wrapping, 239, 241
goals, setting, 10
grilling, 29, 48, 59
guests. See also entertaining
    holiday, 79, 84
    hosting, 47, 84, 233
    shoes, 93
    towels, 145

H

Halloween, 72, 73
Hanukkah, 249
health. *See* wellness
heating and cooling, 55, 207, 208–9, 210, 211
herbs
  dried, 215
  fresh, 54, 64, 220
  planting, 55
holidays. *See also* celebrations; entertaining
  baking for, 23, 52, 76, 84, 242
  cards for, 22, 40, 85, 239
  Christmas, 17, 82, 83, 84, 247–48
  Earth Day, 37
  Easter, 34, 35
  Father's Day, 48
  Fourth of July, 52
  gifts for, 48, 239–41
  guests, preparing for, 84
  Halloween, 72, 73
  Hanukkah, 249
  MLK Jr. Weekend, 19
  Mother's Day, 40
  New Year's Eve, 85
  Thanksgiving, 78–79, 244–45
  Valentine's Day, 22, 23
home maintenance, 204–11
  conserving energy, 208–9
  kits, 209
  patios and porches, 185
  projects and upgrades, 208
  schedules, 210–11
  strategies for, 207
  supplies for, 206
hooks
  adhesive, 11, 101
  for bathrooms, 118
  for bedrooms, 135
  cup, 11, 90, 154
  for kids' rooms, 166
  for kitchens, 98, 102, 104
  S, 11, 140
  for utility spaces, 174, 175
  wall, 11, 89, 92–93
houseplants. *See also* flowers; gardening
  for aromatherapy, 273
  caring for, 18, 55, 199–201
  cleaning, 184, 201
  decorating with, 83, 115, 128, 130, 133, 135
  miniature "forests," 198
  pest control, 18, 201
  schedules, 202–3

I

In-Season Picks, 18, 23, 29, 36, 42, 47, 53, 60, 64, 71, 77, 83
inspiration boards, 154

J

jams, 223
January, 14–19
July, 50–55
June, 44–49

K

keepsakes, 60, 166
kids, 250–59. *See also* craft projects; crafts
  calendars, 253–54
  managing activities, 256–57
  menu planning, 257
  routines, 254, 256
  schedules, 259
  school lunches, 23, 67, 257
  storage, 94, 165–66, 175
  strategies for, 253–57
  study habits, 254–56
  supplies for, 252
  table settings, 241
  traveling with, 259
  workspaces, 152, 168
kids' rooms, 162–71
  arts and crafts, 168–71
  books and toys, 166
  evaluating, 165
  storage, 165–66
kitchens, 96–113. *See also* pantries
  cabinets, 97, 98, 104
  cleaning, 35, 66, 79, 184, 185
  counters, 97, 101
  drawers, 98, 106–7
  evaluating, 98
  islands, 102
  refrigerators and freezers, 108, 113
  shelves, 97, 98, 104
  sinks, 101

L

labeling
  for bathrooms, 118
  for closets, 25, 94, 141
  for kids, 166, 170, 254
  for kitchens, 101, 108, 110
  for laundry, 146, 148, 149
  for offices, 152
  for utility spaces, 174
lamps. *See* lighting
laundry, 186–91. *See also* bedding; cleaning; clothing
  drying, 190
  folding, 145, 190
  hanging, 145, 148, 165, 190
  ironing, 143, 145, 146, 190
  prepping, 189
  schedules, 191
  stains, 145, 148, 189, 190
  strategies for, 189–90
  supplies for, 148–49, 188
  washing, 145, 190
  woolens, 25, 34, 191
laundry rooms, 142–49
  evaluating, 145
  storage, 146–49
  strategies for, 146
  supplies for, 148–49
lawn care. *See* yards
lazy Susans, 11, 101, 104, 110, 118
leftovers
  repurposing, 67, 257
  storage, 106, 108
  Thanksgiving, 79
letters. *See* mail

lighting
for bedrooms, 136
LEDs, 209
for living rooms, 123, 124
for offices, 151, 152, 154
string lights, 27, 248
linens. *See* bedding
living rooms, 122–31
bar carts, 130
bookcases and shelves, 128
cleaning, 184, 185
evaluating, 124
focal points, 124, 131
media centers, 124, 128, 130
seating and accent tables, 127, 131

M

magnetic strips, 101, 111, 152, 174, 208
mail, 90, 92, 93, 159
March, 26–31
Martha Must
apricot jam, 223
buffets, 244
cleaning supplies, 184
closet storage, 138
cookie icing, 34
dusting, 65
fruity cocktails, 235
gardening, 195
garden tools, 25
hardware storage, 208
hydration, 273
ice cream sundaes, 233
ironing boards, 146
junk mail, 159
kids' collectibles, 166

kitchen outlets, 102
knife care, 217
laundry supplies, 190
lilacs, 41
lobster, 58
mailing gifts, 241
miniature "forests," 198
New Year's gifts, 17
orchids, 30
pantry organization, 110
pasta dinners, 49
pesto, 54
phone chargers, 93
potting plants, 201
raw turkey, 78
room layouts, 127
school lunches, 257
sponges, 101
squash, 73, 220
wet clothes, 94
May, 38–43
meal-planning, 65, 218, 245, 257
memory boxes, 166
MLK Jr. Weekend, 19
monthly calendars
January, 15
February, 21
March, 27
April, 33
May, 39
June, 45
July, 51
August, 57
September, 63
October, 69
November, 75
December, 81
monthly tasks
cleaning, 181, 184
cooking, 225

home maintenance, 211
kids, 253, 259
laundry, 191
lawn and garden, 202
pets, 267
Mother's Day, 40

N

New Year's Eve, 85
November, 74–79

O

October, 68–73
offices, 150–61
desks, 152–57
documents, 158
evaluating, 152
filing, 159
technology, 160
ottomans, 11, 116, 127, 131
outlets, 102, 152, 174

P

pantries
cleaning, 66
stocking, 215
storage, 110, 112
papers. *See also* mail
digitizing, 159
document-retention guidelines, 158
filing and sorting, 151, 152, 154, 159
parties. *See* celebrations; entertaining
patios, 185
pegboards, 98, 107, 174
peg rails, 11, 93, 146
pest control

for clothing, 34, 138, 141, 175
for household goods, 174
for plants, 18, 197, 201
pets, 260–67
adopting, 71, 263
bedding, 52, 265
calming, 52
grooming, 264–65, 267
health, 263–65, 267
safety, 267
schedules, 267
spaces for, 263
storage, 92, 94, 110, 173, 263
strategies for, 263–65
supplies for, 262, 263
toys, 264, 265
pickling, 223
picnics, 53
pies, 52, 67, 76, 245
pillows
cases, 25
decorative, 89, 127, 136
down, 145
plumbing, 208, 211
porches. *See* decks
pots and pans, 98, 102, 107
principles of organizing, 10–11
produce. *See also* cooking
gardening, 28, 54, 70, 195, 202
prepping, 218–20
preserving, 222–23
seasonal, 18, 23, 29, 36, 37, 42, 47, 53, 60, 64, 71, 77, 83
storage, 108

projects
    bungee-cord shelves, 154
    command centers, 90
    graphic grid, 168
    home improvement, 208
    kits, 209
purging
    bathrooms, 116, 120
    bookcases, 24, 128
    clothing, 65, 135
    entryways, 94
    holiday decorations, 239
    kids' homework, 259
    kids' rooms, 166
    kitchens, 35, 66, 98, 108, 110
    offices, 152, 160
    tips, 10
    utility spaces, 174

R

recipes and tips. *See also* baking; cooking
    alliums, 31
    apple desserts, 67
    big-batch cooking, 221
    blueberries, 53
    burgers, 48
    cookies, 34, 84, 242
    dried herbs and spices, 215
    for entertaining, 231–33
    flavor builders, 217
    grilled corn, 59
    hamburgers, 48
    handling raw meat, 78
    Hanukkah, 249
    heart-shaped baking, 23
    jams, 223

kitchen scraps, 19
leftovers, 67, 79, 257
lobster BLTs, 58
make-aheads, 231, 242, 245, 249, 257
maple syrup, 29
no-cook meals, 55
nut and seed butters, 217
pasta, 49
pesto, 54
pickling, 223
picnics, 53
pies, 52, 76
produce, freezing, 222
produce, seasonal, 37
rhubarb, 41
roasted squashes, 73, 220
salmon, 217
school lunches, 23, 67, 257
stocks and soups, 19, 66
store-bought broth, 217
Thanksgiving, 244–45
toasted sesame oil, 217
toasting grains, 217
tomatoes, 65, 215
yogurt parfait, 18
repairs. *See* home maintenance
repurposing
    armoires, 130, 152
    baskets, 263
    coffee tables, 168
    for craft supplies, 256
    file sorters, 168
    kids' artwork, 22, 168
    magnetic strips, 208
    maps, 48
    shoe organizers, 168
    spice racks, 118
rugs, 30

S

safety
    air quality, 181
    bunk beds, 165
    cars, 77
    hazardous materials, 174
    home, 76
    pets, 267
screen time, 30, 274
seasonal tasks
    cleaning, 184–85
    cooking, 225
    home maintenance, 210
    laundry, 191
    lawn and garden, 202
    pets, 267
seating
    for bedrooms, 135, 136
    for entryways, 89
    for kids' rooms, 163
    for kitchens, 102
    for living rooms, 124, 127
September, 62–67
sheets. *See* bedding
shelves. *See also* bookcases
    bathroom, 116, 118
    bedroom, 135, 136
    closet, 138, 165
    for craft supplies, 171
    entryway, 93
    for general use, 11
    kids', 163
    kitchen, 97, 98, 101, 104
    laundry room, 146
    living room, 128
    office, 152, 154
    pantry, 110–11
    utility, 174, 175

shoes and boots
    cleaning, 35, 93
    protecting, 76
    storage, 93, 94, 138, 141, 173, 175
    trays for, 31, 93
silverware, polishing, 77
sinks, 101, 116
small spaces, 92–93, 116, 146, 189
sofas. *See* seating
sporting gear, 93, 174, 175, 257
stains
    clothing, 145, 189, 190
    entertaining, 85
    rugs, 30
    supplies, 148, 149

T

tables
    accent, 127
    activity, 165
    coffee, 123, 124, 127
    console, 93
    craft, 168
    kitchen, 98, 102
tag sales, 46
technology
    cords and chargers, 93, 124, 136, 152
    habits, 30, 256, 274
    living room, 124, 128, 130
    office, 160
tension rods, 101, 104, 145
Thanksgiving, 78–79, 244–45
tools
    basic, 206

cleaning, 146, 180

gardening, 25, 194

kitchen, 104, 106, 214

kits, 209

laundry, 146

power tools, 174

towels

bathroom, 116, 118

for cleaning, 93, 94, 265

exfoliating with, 274

folding, 145

for ironing, 146

kitchen, 101, 102

laundering, 61, 189, 190

toys

cleaning, 184

storage, 166, 175

traveling

keepsakes, 60

with kids, 259

kids' kits, 61, 259

plant care while away, 55, 199–201

trays

for bathrooms, 116, 118

for closets, 138

for entryways, 31, 93

general usage, 11

for kitchens, 102, 110

for laundry rooms, 146

for living rooms, 124, 127, 130

for offices, 156, 157

U

upcycling, 118, 154, 168, 239

utility spaces, 172–75

evaluating, 174

storage, 175

V

Valentine's Day, 22, 23

vegetables. *See* produce

vertical space, 94, 104, 128, 146

W

weekly tasks

cleaning, 181, 184

cooking, 225

kids, 253, 254, 257, 259

laundry, 191

lawn and garden, 202

office, 159, 160

pets, 267

wellness, 268–77

bathing, 22, 116

diet, 18, 273–74

exercise, 61, 83, 272

first-aid kits, 271

gratitude, 275

handwashing, 19

healthy habits, 16

holidays, 83

hydration, 60, 136, 273

mindfulness, 274–75

preventative health, 72, 276–77

relaxation, 116

screen time, 30, 274

sleep, 135, 272–73

strategies for, 271–75

sun protection, 43, 274

supplies list, 270

vitamins, 76

windows, 34, 208

winterizing

cars, 72

houseplants, 201

pipes, 211

woolens

laundering, 25, 34, 191

storage, 175

Y

yards. *See also* gardening

bee houses, 54

birds, 19

decks, 31, 85, 207

firewood, 71

improvements, 208

lawn care, 70, 201, 202, 203

snow removal, 72, 85, 210

trees, 76

yearly tasks

cleaning, 181, 185

cooking, 225

home maintenance, 211

kids, 168, 259

laundry, 191

lawn and garden, 202

office, 159

pets, 267

utility spaces, 174

CREDITS AND ACKNOWLEDGMENTS

IMAGE CREDITS

COVER: Lennart Weibull

BACK COVER: Marcus Nilsson

COVER OBJECTS:
Gold Discbound Journal (Martha Stewart for Staples), Mint Linen Deluxe Desk Organizer (Martha Stewart for Staples), Notebook (John Derian), Pencil Tray (HAY)

AKSLAND, DUSTIN: 117

ALLEN, LUCAS: 91

ANDERSON, GIEVES: 263

AVSAR, BURCU: 89

BARBERA, PAUL: 130 (top), 131 (bottom), 167, 230

BERISHA, FADIL: 193, 221, 261

BINDEL, PETRA: 26

BRENNER, MARION: 198

CATHERINE FALLS COMMERCIAL/GETTY IMAGES: 264

CAVANAUGH, CHELSEA: 79, 156 (bottom), 253

COBLE, JACK: 42

COSTELLO, PAUL: 105

DE GRUNWALD, KATYA: 248

DE LEO, JOSEPH: 266

DOLAN, JOHN: 7, 29

DYER, AARON: 23, 40, 49, 72, 73 (right), 78 (right), 85, 155, 170 (bottom), 171, 240

FIELDS, DIANE: 25

FRANZEN, NICOLE: 97

FRIEDMAN, DOUGLAS: 272

GARDNER, BRYAN: 17, 24, 46, 55, 71, 109, 133, 139, 140, 141

HERMAN, GABRIELA: 199

HOM, RAYMOND: 119, 243

HYUP, JONG: 237

ISAGER, DITTE: 53 (right), 103

JOHNSON, STEPHEN KENT: 125

JUELL, ADDIE: 77, 179, 258

KERNICK, JOHN: 54, 74, 202

KIM-BEE, MAX: 134

KUNKEL, ERIN: 246

LAGRANGE, FREDERIC: 28, 205

LIEBE, RYAN: 8, 58, 60, 61

LOFTUS, DAVID: 41 (right)

LOOF, PERNILLE: 22

LOOF, THOMAS: 130 (bottom), 151, 255

LOVEKIN, JONATHAN: 20

MATHIS, KATE: 68, 137, 164, 183, 200, 215, 245

MILLER, JOHNNY: 31, 32, 48, 173, 208, 256

NGO, NGOC MINH: 18, 35 (top), 70, 123, 196

NILSSON, MARCUS: 34, 44, 59, 62, 66, 67 (left), 157 (bottom)

OKADA, KANA: 153, 157 (top)

PEARSON, VICTORIA: 56

PEARSON, VICTORIA/GETTY: 80

PIASECKI, ERIC: 65, 100, 115, 265

POULOS, CON: 52

PUGLIESE, LINDA: 53 (left), 67 (right)

RANSOM, JAMES: 35 (bottom), 95

ROBLEDO, MARIA: 229

ROMEREIN, LISA/OTTO: 126

SCHLECHTER, ANNIE: 99, 106, 107, 111, 170 (top), 251

SCHMELZER, JOE/TREASURBITE STUDIO: 92

SEPTIMUS, MATTHEW: 38

SMART, ANSON: 37

SMOOT, ALPHA: 47

SMOOT, SETH: 78 (left), 156 (top), 161

SOHN, JULIANA: 131 (top)

STRATTON, ANN: 19

STRAUB, THOMAS: 43

TESTANI, CHRISTOPHER: 64, 213, 219, 222

THOMPSON, MARTYN: 234

UCHITEL, DIEGO: 36

ULIN, PIA: 224

VALIANT, JONNY: 144, 169, 175

VANG, MIKKEL: 50, 82

WALKER, JUSTIN: 269

WALLANDER, BJORN: 16, 41 (left)

WEIBULL, LENNART: 2, 4, 187, 216, 227, 232

WILLIAMS, ANNA: 76, 83, 84

WILLIAMS, MATTHEW: 30, 129, 143, 147, 148, 149, 163, 185, 191

WOLKOFF, KATHERINE: 14

YASU + JUNKO: 73 (left), 275

ADDITIONAL CREDITS

TEXT CONTRIBUTIONS BY: Evelyn Battaglia

ART DIRECTION BY: Michael McCormick

This book was produced by

 MELCHER MEDIA

124 West 13th Street · New York, NY 10011 · melcher.com

FOUNDER, CEO: Charles Melcher

VP, COO: Bonnie Eldon

EXECUTIVE EDITOR/PRODUCER: Lauren Nathan

PRODUCTION DIRECTOR: Susan Lynch

DESIGNER/EDITOR: Renée Bollier

ACKNOWLEDGMENTS

MARTHA STEWART AND *MARTHA STEWART LIVING*:

Thank you to our friends and colleagues at *Martha Stewart Living* for inspiring us to be organized in both smart and beautiful ways. Editorial was led by Susanne Ruppert with the invaluable help of Nanette Maxim, Laura Wallis, and Sanaë Lemoine. Contributing editor Evelyn Battaglia proved to be the most organized person we know. Special thanks to Kevin Sharkey for his creative guidance, Ryan McCallister for his gardening expertise, and Thomas Joseph and the MSL test kitchen team for their culinary insight. Michael McCormick is responsible for the brilliant art direction and thoughtful design. We are very thankful to Lennart Weibull, who shot the front cover and many interior images, and to Marcus Nilsson for the back cover, as well as to all the talented photographers listed on page 287. Megan Hedgpeth propped the cover with her usual impeccable style. Special thanks to Kim Dumer, Dawn Sinkowski, Joanna Garcia, Anne Eastman, Sarah Vasil, and Lorie Reilly for their generous contributions. Thank you to our team at Melcher for keeping us organized, ensuring every step was a success, especially Charlie Melcher, Lauren Nathan, Renée Bollier, and Susan Lynch. Finally, we are proud to be partners with Houghton Mifflin Harcourt, working together with Deb Brody, Stephanie Fletcher, and Tai Blanche.

MELCHER MEDIA:

Melcher Media gratefully acknowledges the following for their contributions: Amélie Cherlin, Camille De Beus, Shannon Fanuko, Luke Gernert, Megan Hedgpeth, Samantha Holtgrewe, Liana Krissoff, Ryan McCallister, Ivy McFadden, Jy Murphy, Michael Quinones, Nola Romano, Christopher Steighner, Sarah Vasil, Megan Worman, and Katy Yudin.